...ld   *Arlene Perly Rae*   *Ben Kayfetz*   *Fred Weinberg*   *Edwin Goodman*

...rgov   *Irving Ungerman*   *Ben Dunkelman*   *Joseph Tanenbaum*   *Lou Bregman*

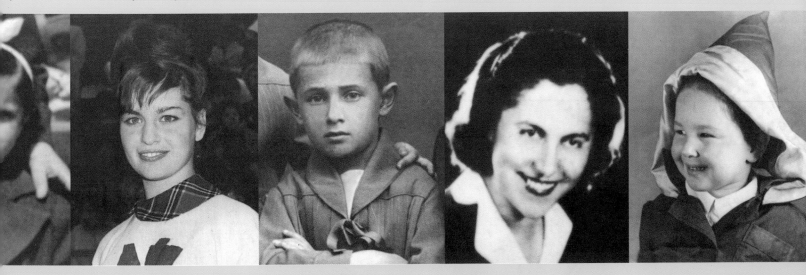

...eck   *Julia Koschitzky*   *Alex Grossman*   *Helen Rodak-Izso*   *Rosie Abella*

GROWING UP JEWISH

These folk tales
are for our grandchildren,
who have been deprived
of the tears, laughter, and
privileges of the immigrant

experience

rosalie wise sharp
spring 1997

GROWING UP JEWISH

Canadians Tell Their Own Stories

Edited by Rosalie Sharp, Irving Abella, and Edwin Goodman

Canadian Cataloguing in Publication Data

Main entry under title:

Growing up Jewish : Canadians tell their own stories

ISBN 0-7710-8058-1

1. Jews, East European – Canada – Social life and customs .

2. Jews, East European – Canada – Biography .   3. Jews – Canada – Social life and customs .   4. Jews – Canada – Biography.   I. Sharp, Rosalie.   II. Abella, Irving, 1940-   .   III. Goodman, Edwin.

FC106.J5G76   1997   305.892'4071   C97-930971-9   F1035.J5G76   1997

Every work in this volume is the property of its respective author.

Previously published works are reprinted by permission.

"Many Are Our Joys," by Edwin Goodman, was previously published in *Life of the Party: The Memoirs of Eddie Goodman* (Toronto: Key Porter Books, 1988). "Room and Keyboard," by Morley Torgov, was previously published in *A Good Place to Come From* (Toronto: Lester and Orpen, 1974).

Book design by K.T. Njo
Layout composition by Sari Ginsberg

The publishers acknowledge the support of the Canada Council and the Ontario Arts Council for their publishing program.

Printed and bound in Canada.

McClelland & Stewart Inc.
The Canadian Publishers
481 University Ave.
Toronto, Ontario
M5G 2E9

1 2 3 4 5   01 00 99 98 97

CONTENTS

—⟩⟨—

Introduction

I n this book are some of the stories — a handful amongst many thousands — that tell of the remarkable Jewish settlement in Canada in the early years of this century. The stories are at once poignant, inspiring, sad, and celebratory, as has been the history of Jewish life in this country.

Who were these men and women who are so lovingly recalled by the contributors to this book? Who were these Bubahs and Zaidahs, these Grandpas and Grandmas? In a word, they were part of an awesome movement of Eastern European Jews, forced out of their ghettos and shtetels some hundred years ago, who arrived destitute but determined in the cities, towns, and farms of Canada and the United States, and who had a dramatic impact on the course of Jewish history.

This mass migration between the 1880s and 1914 drastically changed the face of Jewish Canada. The community became a significant minority in the country rather than a negligible one, increasing from around 2,500 in 1882 to well over 100,000 by 1914. More important than the growth in numbers, however, was the change in composition. By 1914, the acculturated Anglo-Jewish community of Canada had all but disappeared; gone was their serene, comfortable, stable world. In its place had emerged the new world of Canadian Jewry, the seething, crowded, chaotic, noisy, Yiddish world of the Eastern European newcomers.

The immigrants' world was the cramped housing and crowded neighbourhoods of St. John's Ward and Spadina in central Toronto, along the Main (St. Lawrence Boulevard) in Montreal, and north of CPR tracks in Winnipeg. It was a milieu of congested streets, noisy markets, and cramped workplaces; of rag-pickers and junk dealers;

of pushcarts and pedlars; of lines of young and old waiting at street corners before dawn every morning to be picked up by employers who wanted a cheap day's work. Two or three families often shared the same flat, ten or twelve people the same small house, all compet-ing for space with sewing machines and other tools required for piecework done at home. A babel of languages, Yiddish above all, but also Polish, Lithuanian, Russian, Ukrainain, Romanian – everything, it seemed, but English or French – assulted the ears.

Such a world was totally alien to the established Jewish residents of Montreal and Toronto, who were much disturbed by the behaviour and appearance of the immigrants. They were "too conspicuous," complained the rabbi of Toronto's Holy Blossom. How could they successfully integrate into Canadian society? he worried. From the point of view of the established community, the new arrivals were not moving quickly enough to rid themselves of their old European habits. As for their language, to the ears of many of the Establishment, Yiddish was sheer "jargon," its harsh, guttural sounds "grating." The newspaper of the wealthy, the *Jewish Times*, pleaded with the immigrants not to use their language in public.

By European standards, the Main in Montreal, Spadina in Toronto, and Selkirk Avenue in Winnipeg's North End were not true ghettos; people were free to leave and live elsewhere, or so the newcomers were told. But the growing hostility to the immi-grants – from other Canadians – encouraged them to live in a few specific areas. Most were happy to. There, they were among friends, relatives, and townsfolk from their homelands. The food, the smells, the language were familiar. The ghettos of the New World cushioned the shock of arrival in an alien society and allowed newcomers time to recuperate from the trauma of immigration.

These ghettos, for the Jews as for other immigrant groups, provided a breathing space before they and their families were "Canadianized." The immigrant found in the ghetto a historical continuity to his life, a sense of fellowship, a sense of status. In the corner stores, the synagogue, the market, the front yard, kin and friends from home towns in the old country gathered to pass on advice, to gossip, or to decide on whom to send for from their village. As well, they debated the politics of both their new and old homes, talked about working conditions, and organized unions. For the immigrant, the ghetto became his or her anchor in the New World.

The Jewish Establishment discovered to its dismay that it was impossible to impose any order on ghetto life. Just blocks away from their homes was a Jewish world they scarcely recognized and assuredly did not like. They failed to recognize that a communi-ty was taking shape before their very eyes, a community made up of Jews from various countries, cities, towns, and shtetles of Eastern Europe, a community riddled with conflicting ideas, concerns, and ideologies. There were Zionists and anti-Zionists, socialists, anarchists, Yiddishists, secular and Orthodox, each with their own agenda, each with their own plan for the survival of the Jewish people in Canada. The arguments, the noise, and the dissension were often too much for the uptown Jews. How would it look, they wondered, to their Canadian hosts? They feared that the orderly, sedate Jewish society they had worked so hard to create was suddenly bursting apart.

Yet even to the Jewish leadership, it was clear that in the Yiddish-speaking neighbourhoods of Winnipeg, Toronto, and Montreal there was a vitality, a uniqueness, both frightening and inspiring; frightening because with so many conflicting voices it seemed the community would destroy itself; inspiring because of the creativity and energy being generated there.

This generation of immigrants would produce the synagogues, societies, schools, newspapers, theatres, unions, and benevolent organizations that became the foundation of Jewish life in Canada in the twentieth century, just as these products of the ghettos would come to dominate Canadian Jewish society. And their children and grandchildren would make their mark on Canadian society in the areas of business, law, science, finance, medicine, and literature, as have many of those who have contributed to this book.

These waves of Eastern European immigrants were deeply concerned with creating a proper religious life, and almost upon their arrival, tiny new synagogues, called *shtiblach*, sprang up. Each ethnic group, each group of men from the same home town, wanted its own prayer hall to ensure that its unique customs would not be forgotten. By 1914 dozens of *shtiblach* in Montreal, Toronto, and Winnipeg were catering to their own communities. There were Romanian, Polish, Hungarian, Ukrainian, Russian, and Moldavian synagogues. Eastern European Jews who had spent some time in Britain opened up their "Men of England" synagogue. There were synagogues for the men of Minsk, Łagów, Apt, Kiev, Ostrowiecz, and a veritable atlas of Jewish settlements in Poland and Russia.

The synagogues were not simply places to pray. They were social halls, schools, and cultural centres. They united the religious and social life of the neighbourhood and were part of the immigrant's psychological map, his safety net, his security blanket. When all else failed, he knew he would find understanding – if not succour – among his fellow congregants. And outside the synagogue, congregants could mingle, argue, or flirt with the neighbourhood girls.

Almost as important as the synagogue – and, to the secular, *more* important – were the burgeoning fraternal and mutual-benefit societies. Most societies were made up of men and women from the same town or region in the old country. These *landsmanshaftn* were key to integrating the newcomer into Canadian society. An old-timer would take a greenhorn under his wing and find him a home, a job, or even a suitable spouse. And the societies' premises were a place to relax, to play cards. It was another cushioning layer for the immigrant accommodating himself to his new environment.

Though largely isolated from the host society, most ghetto dwellers hungered for news and information both about life in their new country and about the communities they had left behind in Europe. To satisfy this need, the Yiddish newspaper became a staple for every immigrant family, many of whom spoke no English. There were papers from New York, Warsaw, and Berlin, but most popular were those produced at home: the *Kanader Adler* ("Canadian Eagle") in Montreal, the *Kanader Yid* ("Canadian Israelite") in Winnipeg, the *Zhurnal* ("Journal") in Toronto. These were not merely newspapers; for the newcomer they were an introduction to the New World; they were forums of debate, vehicles for self-expression. Stories were reprinted from other Yiddish newspapers all over the world, or translated from the English press. The papers serialized the latest novels and had extensive literary and cultural coverage. They were, for all intents and purposes, the university of the Jewish common man and woman. They were read and reread, savoured and passed around; they provided the ammunition for debate and discussion, reflecting as they did the cacophony of voices and views of the period.

Another phenomenon of the immigrant neighbourhoods was the Jewish bookstores. These did more than sell books and newspapers; they were meeting halls, gathering places where newcomers, students, union organizers, and others could browse through newspapers and books, drink soda water, meet friends and argue. They often also served as lending libraries for those who could not afford to buy books. For many, these stores were an introduction to the wonderful world of Yiddish literature, as well as to the variety of ideologies being debated over seltzer and tea.

Another institution was the Jewish travel agent. Not just a ticket seller, he acted as lawyer, accountant, marriage broker, employment bureau, and pedlar of political influence. His store was the centre of much traffic, as workers came in to put weekly deposits on passages for a wife, child, mother, brother, or sister left behind. While there, the customers arranged for the agent to deal with the police or City Hall over their business licences or their housing problems.

From the bookstores the newcomer graduated to the libraries, the most important, of course, being the Jewish Public Library in Montreal. The library was the community's cultural centre. Around its tables, workers, intellectuals, pedlars, even the occasional boss sat and read and debated — often late into the night — until they were forced out by overworked library staff. The library offered courses on a vast array of topics, sponsored lectures, and brought in authors from all over the Yiddish world.

The ghettos also spawned a vibrant Yiddish theatre, with plays often written and produced by local authors. Montreal had three Yiddish acting troupes; Winnipeg even had its own opera company; while in Toronto Yiddish plays were put on regularly at the Lyric Theatre.

Though most children attended public schools, it was their Jewish education that parents worried about. If their traditions and culture were to survive, if Yiddish was to stand a chance against the compelling pull of English, then the children of the community would have to be educated properly. In the Jewish neighbourhoods of most Canadian cities, the Jewish school system seemed transplanted from an East European shtetl. Following a full day in a public school, instruction was given in *chedarim*, or one-room Hebrew schools. Teachers were mostly failed shopkeepers or men too old or too ill to work in factories. Occasionally these men went door to door to peddle their teaching skills. It was not until various groups began building community-supported schools called Talmud Torahs that a real educational system began to develop.

As on most subjects, the Jewish community was divided on schooling. Some wanted only religious schools; others wanted secular ones. Some thought the language of instruction should be Hebrew; others preferred Yiddish. Some wished the schools to be thoroughly Zionist; others demanded they be socialist. In the end, they all won. As a result of the competing pressures, a variety of night schools was founded, each with its own ideological or religious underpinning.

This, then, was the world of our grandparents, a world this book celebrates, a world worth remembering and savouring, a world worth describing to our children and grandchildren.

PART ONE

A RICH LIFE IN POOR TIMES

*On our way to
Sunnyside, July 1943
(I am on the left)*

A Rich Life in Poor Times

Memories, memories. How fortunate I was to grow up in Toronto in the twenties and thirties. Life was simple and safe then. One cannot escape the past. It shapes us into who we are today. And it always pulls us back. Back to the memories. I grew up in a home with three generations under one roof: grandparents, assorted uncles, aunts, and cousins. There was just one bathroom for all, and hot water only on Friday. Everyone bathed on Friday for Shabbat. The rest of the week we heated water in a kettle, poured it into a basin, and stood shivering in a cold bathroom while we quickly washed ourselves.

Upon arriving home from school on Friday, I was met by the delicious aroma of the Shabbat meal mingling with the clean scent of wax and polish. Everything shone. String mops did not exist yet, so my mother and aunts got down on all fours and scrubbed the floors by hand. Then they covered the surfaces with newspaper, hoping the sparkling floors would remain clean for a day or two.

We had a wood-burning stove in the kitchen that we called "Happy Thought." It had no temperature controls, so one had to put an arm inside it to test the heat level. My grandmother knew the exact order in which to bake all the various foods so they turned out perfectly. By the end of the afternoon

My dad, Joseph Rockfeld (centre), with his uncle Hershel Rosenblat (left) and father, Shea Rockfeld (right)

3

Mom and Dad, on their engagement, 1921

Me in 1928, age 4

she had made challahs, yeast doughs, honey cake, sponge cake, and *kichelach*. It was a labour of love. In an era when women rarely worked outside the home, my grandmother willingly accepted her role as homemaker, as did my mother.

Later on, at the Friday night meal, one of the courses we enjoyed was gefilte fish that had been hand-chopped with a cleaver. More often than not, that fish was so fresh it had been swimming in our bathtub just hours before. No one worried about cholesterol, either. We ate everything that is considered taboo today; shmaltz and gribenas were routine fare. It all tasted so delicious! Despite the amount of fat in our diet, every member of the family was lean, because we walked everywhere.

We observed all the Shabbat rules and even paid a *Shabbes goy* (someone not of the Jewish faith) the fee of one dime to stoke up our furnace in the wintertime. We never turned the lights on or off until after sundown on Saturday, making it truly a day of rest. Locking the door was also unheard of in those days. Friends, relatives, and neighbours simply walked in and announced themselves.

My grandfather *davened* (prayed) in a *shteble* that had about seventy members. Every morning at the crack of dawn he would wend his way to *shul*. He never missed morning or evening services, regardless of the weather. It was his club. It was his life. Immediately after Shabbat services, my grandfather would bring about ten of his cronies home for *kiddush*, the ceremony to sanctify the Shabbat. My grandmother — with some help from me — would prepare herring, *nahit*, and cake. The herring never came from a jar nor the chick peas from a tin. Everything was lovingly prepared from scratch. Everyone would drink *l'chaim* over and over again until they were all completely inebriated. How they enjoyed themselves, pounding their fists on the dining room table in time to the songs they sang.

Saturday afternoons were an "open house" as family and friends gathered at our place for tea. No formal invitation was necessary since all concerned knew they were welcome. No matter how many people showed up, there was always enough food. A huge copper kettle sat on a *blech* (tin sheet), and kept boiling all afternoon. *Havdalah* was also a weekly ritual in our home, and I was the one who got to hold the braided candle. My grandfather always told me to hold the candle high so I would find a tall *chusin* (groom). It didn't work. I ended up marrying a man who was only five-foot-six. Small in stature, but a giant in so many ways.

With Shabbat over, Saturday night was movie night. If I had behaved, I was allowed to accompany my mother to the movies — the highlight of my week. With the purchase of a ticket, each moviegoer was given a dish or a cup and saucer, a practice that allowed many residents in the neighbourhood to accumulate complete sets of dinnerware. Inevitably, during a crucial moment in the movie, someone would drop a dish.

Passover was such a special time in our home, a wonderful family celebration. The women worked so hard preparing for the holiday, scouring every nook and cranny to make sure there was not a crumb of *chometz* (leavened bread) left anywhere. My grandfather then played the inspector, delving into corners with a candle and feather duster, in order to put his stamp of approval on everything. The women pulled potatoes out of hundred-pound burlap bags and grated them by hand to make *kugels* (puddings) during the course of the week. Even the wine was homemade. *Borsht, matzo brei, knaidlach,* and *charoses* were just a few of the delicacies we enjoyed. Because we used only one set of special dishes and cutlery throughout Passover, the menu was limited to *fleishig* (meat) and *parve* ("neutral") foods. Dairy meals were not considered kosher for Passover back then.

During the festive week, all my cousins would gather at our home, and we would each receive a bag of hazel nuts. How grand we all thought we looked in

My parents' best friends, Rose and Louis Garfinkle, and their two adopted daughters, Celia and Sylvia

*Bernard Shimmerman, my
first cousin (seated at left)*

our brand new holiday clothes and shoes! We whiled away the hours by taking turns rolling the nuts down a wooden board propped up against a wall. If your nut hit another, you won all the nuts and a new round would begin.

Rosh Hashana and Yom Kippur were also special times in our home. Yom Kippur was truly a day of awe. Before the holiday we performed the *Shlug Kaporis* ritual, when a live chicken was swung in a circle over each person's head while prayers were chanted. That chicken eventually became our first dinner to break the fast.

Necessity had made my parents thrifty. My mother arranged for the grocer to save some of his sugar sacks for her, which my father then converted

6

into dish towels, aprons, and pillowcases. They *never* wore out. But imagine sleeping on pillowcases that read "granulated sugar." Toilet tissue was another luxury we could not afford. Instead we used the tissue paper that came wrapped around individual oranges in a crate. If you didn't get to the grocer's early in the morning, the wrappers would already have been pilfered by other frugal housewives. My mother smoothed out the tissue and hung it on a nail protruding from the bathroom wall — just one of the many novel systems she devised in order to stretch a dollar.

The age of refrigeration had not yet arrived, so people tended to shop on a daily basis. An ice man made deliveries to keep our icebox stocked. When he chopped away at the chunks to make them the proper size, frozen slivers would fall away, delighting the neighbourhood children, who chased the truck for blocks. Inside the house, it was my job to periodically empty a *shissel* (bowl) under the icebox. Occasionally, I would forget, and the accumulated water would overflow, flooding the kitchen floor.

Horses and buggies delivered all our tea, milk, fruit, and vegetables, as they did to other households. It was common in Toronto to see mounds of steaming manure scattered on the road, which street cleaners cleared with special brushes. The milk we received was non-homogenized, and when the cream rose to the top we would siphon it off to use in our coffee and cocoa. The milk itself came in glass bottles with round cardboard lids that popped up several inches when the milk froze in frigid weather. My mother would purchase milk tickets in advance and leave them in the empty bottles so the milkman would know how many quarts to place inside the double-doored milk cupboard. When we needed cheese or butter we left notes in the bottles as well.

There was also a farmer who called on us once a week to deliver fresh eggs at fifteen cents a dozen. Pre-packaged meats were still far in the future. Our butcher would take out a whole carcass and cut off exactly what we needed. He always threw in liver, lung, and marrow bones — gratis — with each purchase. Choosing a "good" chicken was a real art. My mother would buy a live one, first feeling its bottom to look for a large mound of fat. If it passed muster, she carted it off to the *shochet* (ritual slaughterer), who would slit its throat and toss it upside down into a receptacle to drain the blood. The *shochet* then gave the bird to a chicken plucker to defeather it. But it was back at home that the innards were cleaned out and the laborious job of removing the pin feathers began. We also had to soak the chicken in water and salt to make it kosher.

On our way to Eaton's (left to right: me, Gilda, and Mom)

September 1943

A good chicken soup was dearly appreciated, because we never seemed to get warm enough during the hard winter months. We all vied for a favourite spot next to the boiler that was fuelled by our wood stove in the kitchen. The one lucky enough to get that position would lean their backside against it to warm up temporarily. Instead of the duvets and comforters that keep us warm in bed these days, we used what were called *überbets*, wonderful down-filled covers that my paternal grandmother in Poland sent to my parents along with huge down-filled pillows. It felt so very cosy, as if I had bedded down on top of clouds. Sometimes we heated bricks in the oven, wrapped them in towels and took them under the *überbets* with us to warm our feet. My sister and I also felt the comforting warmth of our parents, with whom we shared a bed. A communal bed may be frowned upon today, but in our day it was common — and we turned out okay.

On Monday nights, before bed, I got to listen to the Lux Radio hour. That hour of pleasure took precedence over everything. I remember listening to it in the dark, imagining all the scenes in my mind. Our main form of home entertainment, however, was playing the phonograph. The machine had to be cranked after every record, but that didn't stop my aunts and their boyfriends from dancing for hours. We also had a piano in the house and often held sing-songs, which I loved. My biggest treat, though, was when one of the several family friends who owned cars came to take me for a drive and buy me an ice cream cone. Such simple things gave us pleasure.

Of course not all our days were filled with joy. Back then, yearly visits to the doctor for a checkup were not yet the norm. Although physicians did make house calls, one only called the doctor if it was an emergency. For most illnesses we had "in house" remedies, such as the sore-throat drink called "goggle moggle," concocted from hot milk, honey, and garlic. It tasted so awful that one stopped complaining for fear the mixture would be administered again. It sure cured you in a hurry. Another remedy for a cough was a mustard plaster: dry mustard mixed with water to make a thick paste, then enclosed in a cloth and applied to one's chest. It really worked!

Public school had eight grades, and the one I attended was called Orde Model School. "Model" because we had both a dentist and a nurse on the premises — very progressive for the times. The dentist checked our teeth every six months, and the nurse visited each classroom weekly, using a wooden tongue depressor to check our scalps for lice. Maintaining good hygiene was not common, and many lice-infested children were sent home to have their hair and scalp washed in kerosene. At school, our lives were very regimented. At ten minutes to nine, when one of the teachers rang the bell, we divided into groups, according to our grade level, and stood at attention. Each group had a captain who announced the group number, at which time we marched silently into our classrooms as a senior pupil played the piano. No talking was allowed. When I reached Junior 2nd (Grade 2), the class graduated from pencil to pen and ink and from printing to script. I remember how excited we were to use our pens for the first time with the ink blotter and pen wiper we had each been given. We carefully wiped the nibs every time we used the pens to prevent rust from forming. But the real privilege was to be chosen as weekly monitor — the one who would clean the blackboards and blackboard brushes.

Even funerals were conducted differently fifty years ago. Mourners followed the hearse on foot, and the lamenting could be heard for blocks. The bereaved allowed themselves to show their emotions and express their grief publicly. When my grandfather died during the first year of my marriage, the *Chevra Kadisha* prepared his body for burial. I clearly remember how the men performed the cleansing and other rituals in a room filled with straw. It was all part of the tradition that played such an important role in our lives. Judaism gave meaning to our days. When I look back, I consider myself enriched by all the experiences I went through. In spite of the hardships, life was indeed joyous. The closeness of family more than compensated for the difficulties we endured.

Phil and I on our honeymoon,
Port Carling, 1946

9

My mother, Harvey, and I in Bronte — Harvey with the big fish I caught

One Foot in the Old World

Growing up Jewish in downtown Toronto was like living with one foot in the new world and one foot in the old — the world from which my parents came. My parents came from Poland (officially as orphans) to a farm school in Georgetown, Ontario.

The Canadian government allowed a number of Jewish orphan immigrants to come to Canada to be trained as farmers. Mr. Morris Saxe was a Jewish farmer who lived in Georgetown, and it was he who came up with the idea of a Jewish farm school. My dad said that they would have starved as farmers, so the orphans all left the farm for the city as quickly as they could.

An American, Mr. Greenblatt, arranged for them to come to Canada. Mr. Saxe co-operated with Mr. Greenblatt to bring fifty-five Polish Jewish orphans, in two separate groups, to Canada in 1927 and 1928. My mom and dad were among the first group of twenty-seven children in 1927. They met on the ship coming over.

Although orphans, my parents were not young enough to be considered orphan children. To be classified as such, you had to be under sixteen. My parents were both eighteen. But because of discrimination by Canadian authorities, this was their only chance to get to Canada. Mr. Greenblatt, who lived in

Sonia and David Goldfarb, newly-weds posing for the postcard picture to send home

Detroit but originally came from Mezritch, the same town that my parents lived in, arranged for my parents' papers to be edited, adjusting their ages downwards by two years. His motivation was to provide opportunity for as many Jewish young people as possible by bringing them to America, which included, in his mind, Canada.

In 1946, after the extent of the Holocaust was exposed, my dad accompanied Mr. Saxe and two other members of the original group to Ottawa in the hope that their group could sponsor Jews to come to Canada from the Displaced Persons camps. They were denied. I remember that he returned from Ottawa feeling defeated and with the impression that anti-Semitism was still government policy. All this is documented in Government of Canada archives, and I have reviewed the documents exchanged between the officials and Mr. Saxe. They demonstrate that anti-Semitism was very much alive, even after the horrors of the Holocaust were known. This has left me with a queasy feeling for Mackenzie King and Louis St. Laurent. They were not magnanimous people; they were, in this respect, prejudiced, weak leaders with little vision.

My parents left the farm school and headed for the city in 1929. My father worked as a cabinetmaker, and one of his jobs was building the showcases in the original Simpson's store in downtown Toronto. My mother worked first as a mother's helper and then in an umbrella factory doing piecework, earning $9 a week (which was significantly more than my father earned at the time, as my mother was inclined to let us know).

During the Great Depression, my father worked, but was only paid sporadically. My mother lost her job. So they took what little savings they had and opened a grocery store at 930 Dundas Street West.

My story begins here. It is the site of the home that my brothers, Stanley and Harvey, and I grew up in. There was a kitchen in the back of the store, which also served as a storeroom; four bedrooms (two on the second floor and two on the third floor); and another kitchen on the second floor.

I remember three families in the household: the Himmelfarbs, with four children, the Grupspoons, with one son, and ourselves. We all lived together harmoniously, although cramped for space. We had the kitchen behind the store; the other two families shared the kitchen on the second floor.

In time, the Himmelfarbs moved, and then the Grupspoons, and one of the bedrooms on the second floor became a living room. By that time we had one bedroom on each of the second and third floors. The second bedroom

*Me and my wagon in the lane
— before store delivery days*

on the third floor was rented to Mr. Jara, a Holocaust survivor, who was supposed to stay with us until his family found another place for him. All I remember is that we only had one bathroom. It was on the second floor and he was always in it.

We ate in the kitchen at the rear of the store, and my mother would always cook a four- or five-course meal that included an appetizer, soup, main course, and dessert. My father would get upset because the store windows would get steamed up. Our menu was varied but predictable. It had a weekly cycle. If the main course was liver, it was Monday; if it was stew, it was Tuesday, and so on. Saturday was the busiest day in the store, so we grazed. On Sunday, we ate upstairs. Sunday, being the only day the store was closed, was the day my mother made a family meal.

We grew up in a house full of love, pride in family, respect for elders, and reverence for education. There was always more than enough to eat, but there was clearly a value in frugality. There was no compromise on books for children or education, but entertainment that was paid for, other than the Saturday movie at the Centre Theatre on Dundas, was rare. Entertainment was

Stan with his little brother Marty

something you did yourself, whether it was games, cards, the schoolyard, free concerts in the park in the summer, or just hanging out. I also remember going to Bellwoods Park, where the Argos would work out. Sundays in the summer, we would go on a picnic.

We also grew up in a house where there was parental self-denial. Children came first. Parenting responsibilities were divided. My mother took care of school and clothes shopping for us, and my dad took care of sports activities. We would arm wrestle or play catch. I have wonderful memories of going to Maple Leaf Stadium with my dad to see the Triple A baseball team – the Leafs – or to the hockey game, where we would buy standing-room grey tickets and race up the stairs to get a spot at the rail (there were always more tickets sold than there were rail spaces).

My dad was a Yankees fan. He listened to Mel Allan on the radio announcing the Yankees' games. He would bet a dollar with Archie Perlmutter, who delivered warm bread to our store twice a day. He and Archie always had a dollar bet on – whether it be on baseball or on hockey, whatever the game, whatever the season. It was good-natured fun.

In our household everyone worked hard, but there was a sense of civility. My father never neglected his sense of decorum; he never left the house without a shirt and tie and a hat. It did not matter what he was doing. He felt that a mark of civility was formality in dressing. My parents' sense of civility also showed in the way they parented. Hitting was out of the question; our parents only had to look at us in a certain manner or speak to us in a certain tone to get our attention.

We had a cat and a dog. The cat's name was Faigalaya, after a friend of my mother whom my dad did not particularly like. Our pets had a purpose, and they stayed downstairs in the store. The cat was there to catch mice, and the dog to bark. When the dog had a dry nose, my mother gave it half an aspirin, the same therapy we were given when we were sick.

Whenever my parents did not want us to know something, they spoke in Polish. My mother generally spoke Yiddish to us, but my father, who rejected everything from his old country, including language, spoke to us only in English. My dad read the *Star* from cover to cover every day. He was Canadian and never looked at a Jewish paper after arriving in Canada.

My mother was an active Zionist and my dad was a socialist. Political subjects were debated; local, national, and international politics were the central subjects of discussion at our kitchen table each evening. The pros and cons of socialism versus capitalism; the political models that allowed for greater opportunity for Jews; the role of Zionism for Israel and in our life in Canada. We were raised to become good Canadians with a genuine sense of our Jewish heritage and were involved in the pursuit of Zionist ideals.

We were a family onto ourselves. We had one cousin that we saw, but as a child I longed for the aunts and uncles that some of my friends had. The *landsman* people from the farm school, who came from the same area of Poland as my mom and dad, were our extended family. We knew each other, helped each other, participated in picnics, and raised money for charity together. This group formed the support structure of our family. They were the people we saw for celebrations or special events.

Our house was gripped with a Depression mentality. The Depression left an indelible mark on my mother and father; saving, frugality, and careful or wise expenditures were always on their minds. My parents felt that it was better to have one high-quality piece of clothing than many inexpensive items.

We were responsible for each other. My brother Stan was a saint. No matter what he did or where he went — whether it was playing in the park or going to a show or hanging out with his friends — he schlepped me along. And I had the same responsibility for Harvey, my younger brother.

Harvey was born a blue baby. I remember the day of his heart operation, which turned out to be a miracle. The neighbours were waiting at the store for my mother to return from the hospital. There was a community anxiety, and it functioned as a support mechanism. And she, true to form, arrived by streetcar, after not sleeping for at least twenty-four hours. We did not own a car, and a taxi would have been extravagant under almost any circumstances. Her own exhaustion was not reason enough to merit the fare.

Harvey was a fantastic kid. I played baseball with him every day in front of St. Agnes's Church. I was determined that he would grow up a normal kid and not spend his time resting, as heart patients in those days were supposed to do. It was my responsibility to take care of him. I was to make sure that his experiences, especially at school, were anxiety free. If he had any difficulty in the schoolyard, or if somebody picked on him in any way, I took care of it. I remember getting into a fight because somebody had stolen an alley from Harvey and he was crying. The principal called my mother, who proceeded to tell him that I was doing what was expected of me; if someone laid a hand on

Harvey, it was my responsibility to make sure that it would not happen again. The principal invited me back to class and the incident was set aside.

The store opened at 7:30 in the morning and closed at 8:30 in the evening. My father would leave for the market by streetcar to buy produce for the store at 4:30 or 5:00 A.M. and was usually back by 9:00 A.M. My mother opened the store, served breakfast, and got us off to school.

Work never ended in the store. Both my parents worked extremely hard and each of us contributed, but, according to my parents, never enough. The fact is that the one who contributed most was my older brother, Stan.

Many of our customers had credit, but the accounts were not by name. Instead they were entered in a book as "Mrs. 20 Grace," "Mrs. 5 Clinton," or "Mrs. 20 Palmerston upstairs." If people did not have money to pay off their credit, which happened on many occasions, my mother would sometimes personally lend them the money. My dad would get frustrated, but she believed that the customers would pay her back, and I think for the most part they did.

We delivered orders in the neighbourhood by bicycle. Some of the customers, we loved to go to, especially on a Friday. I have particularly fond memories of making deliveries to Mrs. Fishstein, who lived on Clinton, just north of College. She baked on Fridays and always gave me a great treat. I also enjoyed making deliveries to my cousin Sheila, who baked great apple pies. Then there were the customers at the other extreme, the ones who sent bottles back in the dead of winter, when it was difficult, uncomfortable, and even dangerous to carry them on your bike.

I decided to save paper, enough for a bicycle. My brothers and I collected the paper from customers who had agreed to save it for me. I stored the paper in an old shed (which we called a chicken coop, likely because chickens were once kept there) behind the store. Two years' worth of saved paper was enough to buy a third of a bike. With my paper, and money from my parents, I finally got my bike – a Raleigh Racer. It was a great bike. Times were difficult. Money was precious!

We used to deliver a basket of peaches for five cents' profit. We would ask for the basket to be returned, because we would sell it back to the farmer and make as much money on it as on the peaches.

Religion and religious observance were not fundamental to our life. We did not belong to or attend a synagogue, but our house was kosher. We did not make it easy for mother to keep kosher, however, because we always made mistakes. But if we used a dairy fork for meat, she had a simple solution: she buried the fork in the earth of a houseplant for twenty-four hours, and the fork would be kosher again. It was an efficient solution for a lot of mistakes.

I went to the Yeshiva Toras Chaim, which was at Montrose and College, from the time I was nine or ten until I was thirteen. It was better known as the Yeshiva Torture Chamber. The school was in a building attached to a synagogue that had been converted from a church. The institution had no genuine interest in me as a student, as my parents were not members of the synagogue and neither did they attend. I did not learn much, but we had a lot of fun. Hebrew school was a place for frivolity. We had little respect for the education process, the teachers, or anything to do with the place.

I went to the Yeshiva to prepare for my Bar Mitzvah. I do not believe my dad, a non-believer, really cared, but my mother was determined that each of us would have a Bar Mitzvah. I clearly remember the party. It was in our home on a Sunday, and a special guest, Mr. Saxe, came. This was a very special honour for my mother and dad. I was to make a speech that others had written, but when the time came, I refused to make it, and instead delivered my own simple but appropriate speech.

We went to Grace Street Public School and then Harbord Collegiate. My mother referred to the latter as Harbord Collision. We went to school no matter what. To miss school was the ultimate sin. I remember the snowstorm of 1944, when we were marched off to school even though there was no hope of getting there. For us, life was quite simple; if we did well in school, life at home was quite easy. Teachers were revered, beyond reproach by us, even if my mother sometimes intervened on our behalf.

My mother was an extremely dedicated parent. At one parents' night, my math teacher told her that I was not fit for school. She proceeded to tell the math teacher that she had come to school to find out why he was such a lousy math teacher, and suggested that the two of them go to the principal's office. After that I never had trouble with that teacher again.

Me as a Zionist Kwakiutl Indian

My mother was street wise, and played along with our teasing. We would tell her that in terms of grades, A was awful, B was bad, C was crummy, D was damn good, E was excellent, and F was fantastic. She went along with the gag, but if your report card was not good, you had to deal with her disappointment, and the burden of disappointing her was one of the worst feelings you could ever experience.

Life in my teens was great. Harbord Collegiate was an exciting place to be. Life centred around school, sports, and occasionally helping in the store. I played basketball at school. My parents were never that enthusiastic about my involvement in sports, because they felt it would undermine my commitment to education. My parents said there were three things in life for a teenage boy: school, sports, and girls. I was allowed two, and one had to be school. Sports for me were most important; the Y at Bloor and Spadina was central to my life. But this was a place for sports *and* girls. Friendships forged there were for life. I knew deep down, however, that school was preeminent; education was essential for an acceptable quality of life.

We were raised in a family where community involvement, most often defined as the Jewish community, was important. My parents participated in raising money for Pioneer Women, sending packages to Palestine, later Israel, and volunteering. Community responsibility was fundamental.

Our neighbourhood was Italian and Jewish. Our store was a lane and a store removed from St. Agnes's Church. The priest was a customer of ours, and I would deliver orders to the church residence two or three times a week.

My dad got along well with everybody. In fact, so well that when a group of young men decided to rob our store (there was a poolhall attached to the church), a young fellow came to tell him to take the family out because the store was about to be robbed. We went to the park and the store was robbed, but little was taken, because there was nothing there.

I played hockey for Columbus Boys Club, which was mainly for Catholic boys on Bellwood Street, south of Dundas. Carmen Bush was the coach and a wonderful person. For the most part, there was little prejudice from my team mates.

Neighbours helped each other. I remember once running away from camp. My father came to get me and take me home with Roy Rubinoff, who owned a gas station. Roy Rubinoff had a car, and in an emergency he, as driver, and his car were at the neighbourhood's disposal.

My wedding to Joan, on June 7, 1960

It seems to me that life was more generous then. People were more sensitive to each other. There was a respect and a give and take and a sharing that does not exist today, and I think neighbourhoods today are less successful because of it. People learned to accommodate each other, because there was an understanding that some day they might need each other.

After my brother Harvey was operated on, Dr. Gordon Murray told my mother to take him to the country for the summer and that the money we owed him (his fee in the days before OHIP) should be used to rent a cottage. So my brother Stan and my dad stayed home to run the store, and I went off to a cottage in Bronte with my mother and Harvey.

I remember my mother having an argument with our next-door neighbour at the Bronte cottage who had made some anti-Semitic remarks. The neighbour's name was Mr. Sergeant. My mother never took a back seat to anybody, and proceeded to blast him. Mr. Sergeant was part of a small community of fishermen in Bronte, and after his run-in with my mother, he brought her fresh fish every day in an attempt to make up.

Our home was a traditional home. Frugality, respect for elders, no swearing, responsibilities both at home and in the store, these were the standards of behaviour we were expected to live by. In some ways we grew up in an atmosphere of European conservatism. There was, however, one exception: Vincent.

My mother had always had weekly cleaning help, and Vincent came to clean once a week for many years. Vincent was a transvestite. He arrived at our home dressed as a man, in a neat black suit, a shirt and tie, and a hat (because he was bald). But he always cleaned dressed as a woman, wearing high heels, a skirt and blouse, and a kerchief.

Vincent was a decent, honest, honourable, and generous person. He became a friend of the family, and my parents accepted him as he was, without prejudice. At Christmas, my mother would always give him what he wanted: women's lingerie. Their acceptance of Vincent was typical of their attitude of fair play. My brothers and I had a relationship with him no different than with anyone else; we grew up with him and never thought there was anything strange or out of the ordinary about him. Indeed, only after I was grown up did I learn the word "transvestite" or realize it was at all unusual to believe that housework was always done in women's clothes!

There are many forms of wealth, and for me one of the most important was the care and affection that we received daily from our parents. I learned to be independent and tough from my parents. My dad was interested in sports, international affairs, and politics. My mom was interested in education, charity, and economic success. I inherited my drive for business from my mother and my love of politics from my father.

Our family was not without tension, but had enormous love, and both my parents were clearly role models. Canada was important to them. They loved their adopted country and felt honoured to be here. Even later in life, they had no interest in returning to Poland for a visit.

We were raised to believe we were strong and independent. Once, the school nurse sent me home with a note suggesting that I had allergies. My

The family today (standing, left to right: Rebecca, Michael, Alonna, Martin, Joan, Baila. In front, left to right: Avi, Daniel)

mother promptly sent me back to school with another note that said that our family did not have allergies, only an occasional rash.

My dad was fundamentally a socialist and never wanted to be in business. He was driven into it by my mother. My mother was an entrepreneur, charitable and determined that we, her children, would succeed through education. I am one of those lucky ones who had great parents. My mother was kind, sympathetic, and generous to a fault. I could do no wrong in her eyes. My dad was as proud, but was less able to show his emotions. He was able to express his love for his grandchildren far more freely.

Dundas and Grace is also my heritage. Downtown Toronto left its mark on who I was and who I continue to be.

The Chicken store at 192 Baldwin Street (top left, my brother Abie)

JOE BERMAN

The Jewish Indian Chief: A True Story

Joe Berman (centre) in the Royal Canadian Navy, c. 1943

To tell the story of the genuine Jewish Indian chief my uncle and I happened to meet deep in the Canadian wilderness of 1937, I must go way back and begin my tale nearly twenty years earlier in Europe after the First World War.

Family lore describes how my parents arrived in Toronto. In 1919, my father, the eldest child of eight, left his village, Estrapolya, in Ukraine, to avoid pogroms and to evade the fighting between Tsarist troops and the Communist army during the height of the Russian Revolution. His family traded in farm animals, primarily horses, supplying the military and farming establishments. Their business took them as far as Odessa, to markets that attracted many merchants from far beyond those borders. In order to communicate with his vendors and customers, my father learned to speak three or four languages fluently.

A younger brother, Max, was already living in Canada, having emigrated before World War I. In keeping with the Jewish custom, Max worked, saved his money, and sponsored one relative at a time to join him. It was my uncle Max who provided a "ship's carte" for my father, a prepaid ticket for ocean passage, which was waiting for him in Antwerp. (All the necessary paperwork was done by an agent in Toronto – a Mrs. Dworkin – who had an office on Dundas Street, just west of Spadina.) Travelling was a chaotic affair back then, and

Russian money was worthless outside the country, even if you were lucky enough to have some. So my father decided to walk across Europe to get to Antwerp. On the day he arrived in Lemberg (now Lvov, Poland), he met my mother, Miriam, later known as Mary. She was from a nearby village, where she had been born, raised, and educated, unlike most Jewish young women of the time, who received no formal education. But this particular area, part of the Austro-Hungarian empire under the reign of Emperor Franz Joseph, was quite enlightened. Miriam also came from a merchant family that traded across international borders, finding markets in several different ethnic states of the empire. As a result my mother spoke nine languages fluently. When my father arrived in Lemberg, my mother was working as a teacher. The two married there and, because of the tough living conditions, decided to push on together toward Antwerp on foot. They finally reached their destination in the fall of 1920, and somehow managed to arrange for my mother to accompany my father on the designated ship. The young couple sailed in steerage to Quebec City and from there took a train to Toronto. But their final destination was rural Elmira, a small town just twelve miles outside Kitchener, Ontario (which had recently been renamed from Berlin, Ontario).

By 1937 we were living in Toronto, and I was fifteen years old – the eldest of six children. We lived in the heart of Kensington Market, the Jewish commercial district, right on Baldwin Street. My parents subsisted by selling live chickens to Central European immigrants. Most, but not all, of their customers were Jewish. Our store was at the front of the house, with a kitchen /all-purpose room forming a connecting passageway between the storefront and the holding sheds out back. My father would leave the city on Monday mornings at 3 A.M. and drive to Elmira, where he would do business with the area's Mennonite farmers. He would buy their two-legged yard animals: chickens, ducks, and geese, and turkeys when the season dictated. By Tuesday night or Wednesday morning, when he had about 100 to 150 crated birds loaded onto his truck, my father would head home. He would transfer the squawking birds from the truck to a shed behind our house, where they would bide their time until Thursday, when the Jewish homemakers arrived to make their purchases.

Each customer would buy a live fowl, then take it down the street to the *shochet*, a specially ordained religious man who would perform a ritual slaughter. The women would then pluck the feathers off the dead bird and take it home, along with their freshly purchased fish and vegetables, to prepare the Jewish Sabbath meal. Business for us stopped slightly after noon on Friday — since Saturday was the holy day and Christian Toronto's "blue laws" prevented business transactions on Sunday — so we used the day to clean out the chicken coops and holding sheds in the backyard. The only rest for Jewish families in those days was the Sabbath and the High Holidays. Later, as the Jewish community moved away from strict observance, even that day of rest vanished. Despite the pressure on all siblings to join in making our family living, my brothers and sisters all completed high school, and, with help from them all, I was fortunate enough to attain a degree in physics and engineering at the University of Toronto.

But back to my tale, and the scenes that form the background of the picture I am painting. Although we were closed Sunday, the boys of the family were kept busy cycling to customers' homes to collect on the credit that had been advanced the Thursday before. This was a necessary routine, because income earners at that time received their salaries only on Friday afternoons. As mentioned, the women shopped on Wednesday and Thursday, by which time the entire previous week's pay had already been spent. That bicycle route gave me a good overview of the geography of the city's Jewish community. But many were the Sundays when no money could be collected because the

*My mother, Mary, inside
the store on Baldwin Street*

workers of the family were on strike and flat broke. During the late 1920s, Toronto's labour unions were beginning to organize. Almost every day at noon, and again at five o'clock, powerful speakers would hold sway in the open air outside the Labour Lyceum and at the main working-class corners on Spadina Avenue – at Queen, at College, and at St. Andrews.

We boys also had another cycling routine. After school and after religious school and Hebrew lessons, we would use our bikes to deliver chickens and eggs to customers whose husbands had dropped by to place orders on their way to work. Then, before anyone had private telephones, we became the first modern business with a phone, sharing it with non-competing storekeepers. When we took phone orders for our customers, we also took their orders for bakery, meat, fish, fresh produce, and grocery products. Then we delivered the goods on our own rounds as a courtesy to our customers, with no extra charge.

At that time my uncle Louis, my father's brother, was a cattle driver whose trading area covered the territory of northern Quebec in the fertile Clay Belt region. It was the height of the 1930s Depression, and the government had managed to open up this area by offering free land to French-Canadian families who were on the dole. The program gave each family an axe, a two-handled swede saw, a cow, some seed, and possibly a horse and plough. In return, the family was expected to clear the rocks and trees from their plot of land, plant seed, and harvest a crop. The soil was very productive, made up mostly of deeply layered topsoil over a rocky undersurface, and the recipients were expected to keep adding cleared land to their holdings each year. The region was accessible only by gravel roads from Montreal and Ottawa and by a rail line that operated once a week to the newly established pioneer towns of LaSarre, Tachereau, and Amos. The farms themselves were reachable only by horse and buggy or high-axled Model A Ford trucks.

Uncle Louis would arrive each spring and stay through the summer until the High Holidays in early fall. He travelled the back roads buying four-legged farm animals — cows, bulls, sheep, and sometimes swine. He would give each farmer a cash deposit and withhold the balance of payment until the animals were successfully delivered to one of the three isolated railway depots. The livestock then embarked on their three-day railcar journey all the way to the Toronto stockyards at Keele and St. Clair. There, they were auctioned to the farmers of Southern Ontario, who continued to fatten them up on the range during the fall, and in cosy barns over the winter. Purchasers from the packing house located next to the stockyards also bid in those early fall auctions. My uncle's profit margin — and livelihood — depended on the risky business of estimating the future price of beef and the weight the animals would gain from the time he bought them in Quebec to the time they were auctioned in Toronto.

Now that I have outlined the second element of this unlikely painting, it is time to sketch in the third: blueberries. Around the same time my uncle was trading in livestock in Quebec, it was wild blueberry season around North Bay, Ontario. The berries were picked in the bush, then trucked in baskets to the Toronto market. But in the summer of 1937, there was a severe drought and few blueberries to be picked, causing prices to skyrocket. It just so happened that my uncle invited me to accompany him on his summer voyage through the backroads of our young country. Once in the Quebec bush, we saw that the blueberry crop there was both ripe and abundant. My uncle knew a good opportunity when he saw one, but was unsure how to capitalize on this potential. Locals told us that a nearby Indian tribe always picked that crop of berries, and they pointed us toward their village, which was forty miles farther into the bush on an old logging road that was negotiable only by a high-axled vehicle. We now had a plan of action.

Eventually we arrived at a clearing where a collection of shacks and lean-tos formed the Indian village — a far cry from the quaint tepee towns of Hollywood fable. The chief's residence was off to one side, no different from any other shack except for a deerskin flap hanging over the entry in place of a door. We called out hesitantly that we wanted to speak to the chief in order to arrange a business transaction. The chief bid us enter. Although the sun was shining brightly outside, we entered into a dark interior, where we could make out a figure squatting on the earthen floor, wearing a weatherbeaten jacket and pants and a leather slouch hat. Uncle Louis spoke to the Indian in a sort of pidgin French that he had picked up over the years. He stated our business and indicated that we would supply the baskets — made in town from birch bark — and would pay a certain number of pennies per basket of blueberries delivered to the nearest railhead. The chief countered with twice as much money, and we haggled down to an amount midway between — all laboriously negotiated in this pidgin language. Finally, my uncle put out his hand and said, "It's a deal." At the same time, the chief extended his hand and said, "It's a deal, *landsman*." Uncle Louis and I looked at each other in shock, because *landsman* is a Yiddish word used by Jews to identify themselves to fellow members of the community. Its literal translation from the original German is "fellow countryman." Neither my uncle nor I wanted to pursue this strange turn of events any further. Frankly, we thought we hadn't heard him correctly. And if we had, we feared embarrassing the chief, in case he had picked up a foreign word and then used it incorrectly. We were about to leave, when the chief said in perfect English, "Are you not going to ask me why I used the word *landsman*?" After telling him our reasons for not pressing the matter, he said, "Please sit down and I will tell you an interesting story."

"My name is Ginsberg," said the Indian chief. "I live in Montreal, where I have a fur factory that turns animal skins into fur coats. I come to this countryside every spring to buy the furs that these Indians trap during the winter. This is their only cash crop, and they depend on it for their livelihood. I had been doing this for many years and have come to know them fairly intimately.

"In the early 1930s the government decreed a ban on trapping beaver, the most important fur animal in this area. The ban was well enforced by the RCMP, the only police force in the district. The law not only prohibited trapping beaver, it also prevented trading in beaver fur, meaning the tribe had no cash to buy their provisions, and I, of course, had no beaver fur for my plant.

This continued for several years before it occurred to me that, as a Montrealer, I could easily go both to Quebec City and Ottawa to see if I could get some relief from this edict.

"To make a long story short, I was eventually successful and obtained a document from the RCMP exempting this tribe from the ban. As a result of my actions, the tribe elected me Honorary Chief for all negotiations with the government, the police, and with outsiders coming to do trade. So that is how I came to be Ginsberg – The Indian Chief."

There you have it, a true story that defined for me the summer of 1937, and completes my portrait of a few Jewish lives in Canada at that time.

Bill Gold, age 22

><

Playing on the Sandlots

Long ago, in the dim and distant past, 1905 to be exact, my parents, five of my brothers, two sisters, and I arrived in Toronto. We had started in Russia, then, after spending a few years in London, England, we sailed for Canada. I was the only child born in England and was six months old when we arrived in Toronto. I remember asking my father several years later, "Why did we come to Toronto, Canada?" He said, "That was where the bus stopped. Besides, where else would a cabinet maker go but to a big city?" The family's residence back in London was on Abbott Road above a barbershop. Three of my brothers became barbers. Our flat had two bedrooms for the ten of us. Our home in Toronto was on the southwest corner of Anderson Street and University Avenue, now University and Dundas. I started my rather short schooling at Orde Street Public School – which was then located on Orde Street just south of College, between McCaul and University – and finished my schooling at Wellesley Public School, because Orde Street didn't have a Grade 8.

The main occupation for the young children of an immigrant family was sports of every description. Fortunately for me, I was athletically inclined and could make my way on the streets by playing baseball with a little boxing mixed in. It is interesting for me to recall how popular baseball was in Toronto

My father, Max, 1906

31

My mother, Marsha, 1906

at the turn of the century, long before there was a Canadian team in the major or minor leagues. In the cities of North America, with their ghettos of Italians, Jews, blacks, and other European nationalities, one way for the young people to get ahead was through sports. The child's world consisted of sports and the city playgrounds, and my own world was made up of the friends, heroes, and wonderful people I met through sports.

Fortunately for the young Jewish teenagers, we had plenty of Jewish heroes, especially at the Lizzie playground under Bob Abate. But until the early twenties, the top Jewish baseball team, the Judeans, had the odd Christian who sneaked in and played for them. Fortunately for me, I was well co-ordinated, and when I was fourteen I played for Lizzies at second base. By the time I was twenty-two, David Dunkelman of Tip Top Tailors, who sponsored a baseball team, needed a second baseman badly. They were supposed to field only employees, so I was given a job and Dunkelman's had a new second baseman. I was earning $21 a week, and believe me I felt I had struck it rich. I was able to contribute to the family income, and we thought we were in clover.

In softball the Jews had a championship senior team, due in large measure to the pitching of Harry Sniderman, Carol Grafstein's father, who was not only a great pitcher but also the toughest competitor in the league. In those days the teams survived on getting part of the gate, and the players got a cut. Harry made certain that the Herzl Zions got their fair share. We had a great team and were champions for several years.

My older brothers decided if I was doing so well in baseball I should try boxing. Charlie Ring ran the Newsboy Boxing Tournament, which I won in the featherweight class. I was also runner-up in the Ontario tournament. I thought I was doing great at boxing until I was hammered in one fight and my brothers decided I should stick to baseball.

The Jewish community, however, had some great boxers during the teens and twenties. Sammy Goodman became the Canadian flyweight champion while at university and was going to go to the Olympics until his mother decided it was not for a Jewish boy and intervened. Sammy could kick a football farther than anybody in the country and played with the great Lionel Conacher.

Other great Jewish boxers of those days included Phil "Scotty" Lisner, Harry Freeman, and Benny Gould, a welterweight champion. In the thirties there were the two Yacks and Sammy Luftspring. Sammy was ranked No. 3 lightweight in the world and was on his way to becoming the world champion when he was blinded in one eye in a fight and had to give up boxing. He became a club owner and entertainer.

While the men starred in the early days, the ladies were no mean shakes. Bobbie Rosenfeld was undoubtedly the best Canadian woman athlete in the first half of the century. She played hockey, baseball, basketball, and was also a runner at the 1928 Amsterdam Olympics, where she won a silver in the 100m dash and a gold in the 4 x 100m relay. She was the darling of the sportswriters, and you could not read a sports page without seeing her name. The other Jewish Olympic medal winner in the twenties was Hank Ceiman, the great heel-and-toe walker.

In the early thirties the Cleveland Supremes, the American baseball champions, came to play the Lakeside Ladies, starring Bobbie Rosenfeld. The Toronto team won, which was regarded as a great victory for Canada.

In basketball in the twenties and thirties, the Jewish teams, both men and women, were always near the top of the league, with Neumee Eisen and Harold Sniderman, both of whom played on the Lizzies' junior team, and Bobbie Rosenfeld among the most prominent. The Lizzies won many titles on the Toronto and Ontario levels, and in 1929, in Woodstock, New Brunswick, won the coveted Canadian title. It was a tremendous victory for the Toronto playground. Others on the team included Harold (Skinny) Gallander, Alex Levinsky, Yudy Mincovitch, and Lefty Starr. The mainly Jewish Harbord Collegiate also produced some great basketball teams.

The breaststroker Shier Mendelson was one of the best known figures in the Jewish community, winning many national and international swim meets in the 1920s. At the time he was Canada's greatest swimmer, and he trained many of Ontario's best swimmers, including George Young.

In football the Jewish community in the early days did not do as well, although Moe Shatz was a great varsity star and Harry Sonshine was an all-Canadian. Curly Lewis played for Balmy Beach with the great Teddy Reeve, and Harbord Collegiate won a City championship in 1935 with a mostly Jewish team.

One of the best all-round Jewish athletes was Alex (Mine Boy) Levinsky. He was the only Jew in pro hockey, playing defence for the Toronto Maple Leafs when they won the Stanley Cup Championship in 1932. In later years he was traded to the New York Rangers and then to the Chicago Black Hawks, where he was again on the cup-winning team in 1938. Levinsky was also a

Me, in 1933, the year I got engaged

My wife-to-be, Lillian Gallander

With Lil on our sixtieth wedding anniversary in 1994

wonderful baseball player, and was a member of the Lizzies basketball junior team that won the Canadian championship. Another excellent all-rounder was my brother Sammy, who also played hockey, baseball, and basketball. He played for many prestigious teams, including the Beavers at Perth Square, and once went on a barnstorming trip with the Oslers, which all resulted in a great, well-paying job playing for the CPR.

My job at Dunkelman's was certainly not the beginning of a great career for a young man with an elementary school education. Furthermore, I wanted to get married. Fortunately for me and other athletes, the brewery business recognized our worth as sales representatives and in public relations. I went to work for Carling and visited all the hotels and public houses, pushing their products. This gave me a good knowledge of the hotel and public house business, which had always fascinated me because I liked and knew a lot of people. While playing for the breweries, Jersey City, of the International Baseball League, offered me $1,700 to play out the rest of the season with them. I turned them down.

I fell in love with the beautiful Lil Gallander, and we got married and had two lovely daughters. All the Gallander girls are beautiful. Lil's father, Benjamin Gallander, came to Canada in 1901 from Poland. His wife, Ida Farber, who remained behind for seven years until he was able to send for her and the rest of her family, was the oldest of eleven children. The Farber families just grew and grew, and I used to think every Jew in Toronto was related to the Farbers. In the 1980s they had a meeting of the cousins and over three hundred people showed up. It was a wonderful party.

After a few years I left the brewery business, and Earl Torno, whose family was in the wine business, and I bought the Avonmore Public House, then the Stafford, and finally, a real hotel, the Barclay on Front Street. Until I retired, the hotel business was my life. As you grow older, and I guess ninety-one is old, you have a tendency to look back and enjoy your memories. Some of my very happiest memories are of playing on Toronto's sandlots. Sports provided the greatest entertainment, but they also kept us out of trouble and taught us lessons about friendship and fair play we have carried with us our entire lives.

Lillian's parents, Benjamin and Ida Gallander

*My mother, Hannah Florence
(centre), with brother Harold
and sister Ruth*

ARLENE PERLY RAE

A Tale of Two Families

My Zaida and Zero Mostel told the same joke. There was a little town near the Russian-Polish border. (Was it his town, Radom? Or Lodz, where my Bubby's family came from . . . ?) From war to war, control alternated between Russia and Poland for decades. An old man was asked, "Which of your occupiers did you prefer?" His answer was clear: "The Poles, definitely." Then he explained, "Who can stand those awful Russian winters?"

Around 1911, sensing bad times coming, my father's father, Saul Perelgut, left Poland. He chose "Hamilton, America," because he knew someone there, a Mr. Boxingbaum. He was clearly a longtime friend – his photograph dots our oldest family album. Saul left a family dry-goods store in Radom. I have been to Poland and noticed that the industrial, steel-based area is, even today, not unlike Hamilton.

He sent for his wife, Rebecca, and four sons a year later. Rebecca's family name was Wizen. Family lore claims it was actually Wizel, but they were inexplicably forced to change it. The boys were Phillip, Morris, Joe, and Albert. Albert was (then) the youngest, one and a half at the time. Supervising four rambunctious boys aboard ship was challenging to say the least. One day little Albert went missing. General panic ensued, led by my Bubby's hysterical cries,

My paternal grandfather, Saul Perelgut, sitting in front of his store, Modern Paint & Wallpaper, in Hamilton

37

until the inquisitive toddler was found. She never let him — my future dad — out of her sight for the rest of the journey.

Saul learned to paint and hang wallpaper. He purchased a wagon, paint, and a ladder, and every day walked three miles across town from their Cannon Street flat to Ottawa Street. His pitch was simple — he'd paint any room for $10. Apparently there were takers, for a few years later, around 1917, he opened a store beside the Fisher Hotel. Soon he bought a building with a bigger store, Modern Paint and Wallpaper, on York Street (now a mall). My uncle, Harry Perell, the fifth (and sole surviving) son, the only one born in Canada, was six. He has scant memory of the first store, but recalls the excitement of the move. After his military service, Harry ran the business successfully for years. I remember the store, too, a long room with reams of wallpaper, tons of paint-cans, and those wonderful mixing machines that shake like crazy and make a tremendous noise enjoyed by all children.

The cost of the building in 1927 was $10,000. After Saul's deposit, interest on the rest was at 6 ½ per cent. Various fees were: tax certificate, fifty cents; title investigation, ninety cents; registration, $2.45; searching executions, thirty cents; bankruptcy search, fifty cents. Land transfer tax was steeper, $20; legal fees, a whopping $50.

Rebecca, happy and outgoing, adapted quickly to Canada. She was chosen secretary of the *shul*, because she soon spoke and wrote English better than anyone else around. The boys attended school and helped at the store. My dad, Al, picked up the nickname Perly, and later chose it officially as his surname. Morris kept Perelgut, the others adopted Perell. As a teenager, Al sold two newspapers, the *Herald* and *Spectator*, at the corner of King and James, apparently a first rate location.

With the Depression, family fortunes actually improved. Unemployed men were desperate to do odd jobs, painting among them. Saul's business did better than expected, selling them supplies. Not trusting banks, Saul kept a safe with a few thousand dollars at the back of the store. During those difficult years, he frequently made loans to friends and neighbours. He charged no interest, accepting people's word of honour that they would repay him when they could. Everyone did. Some of these "get by" loans were to members of what are now among Hamilton's most prominent families. For years afterwards, Saul and his sons were occasionally approached for (understandably popular) free loans. Morris developed a standard reply:

"We've now made a deal with the bank. They won't sell paint if we don't give loans."

The family moved to a bigger house on Hess Street and purchased three other properties on the same block. Tenants who couldn't pay rent were encouraged to fix up their houses instead.

My father was a bit of a daredevil. He and kid brother Harry shared a bedroom. In one roughhousing session, they accidentally broke their brother Joe's arm and hid in a wardrobe to escape their furious father. Joe, who grew up to be a dignified and intelligent man, taught math for years at Delta Collegiate. He became Supervisor of Mathematics for the Hamilton Board of Education. He married a Christian woman, my elegant Aunt Muriel, a buyer for Fosters. Their union was barely acknowledged by my grandparents and they did not visit each other's homes for years. Joe and Muriel had no children. They lived with their dog, Stinky, in a beautiful ravine-backed house in Burlington. There were trilliums out back and great bird watching. The brothers and their families remained close, and my grandparents' hearts eventually softened.

My dad refused to become Bar Mitzvah; he disliked the rigidity of the rabbis. Even his Hebrew lessons were bizarre. Avoiding the teacher, he lurked on the far side of the large desk. Hebrew is strange enough; an ancient script, no vowels, and moving from right to left. For years, as a sort of party trick, my dad could also read it upside down! Not surprisingly my Jewish upbringing in Toronto was decidedly Reform.

Once, on a dare, Al, a strong swimmer, swam across Hamilton Bay. Another time, at nineteen years old, he jumped on a train loaded with hoboes. When he phoned – from the prairies – his frantic parents demanded he return home immediately. Al did, and sold his story to the *Spectator*: "Travelling across Canada Courtesy of the CNR."

Al was a terrific rower, and at twenty-six was a key member of the Leander Rowing Club. The team qualified to represent Canada at the 1936 Olympics. Since he was Jewish, Al was urged by Canadian officials not to attend the games in Berlin. He stoically complied.

Al was also very sociable; many stories revolve around dating adventures and setting up friends. He made many matches. I still meet couples who admit my late father brought them together. His first wife, Jean Geller, died giving birth to a daughter, Jeannie. In 1946 he married my mother, Hannah Florence.

Al and Hannah Perly (centre), on their wedding day, outside Holy Blossom Temple in Toronto, April 7, 1946. Flanking them are Hannah's parents, Mira and Meyer Florence.

My father, Al Perly (centre), with members of the Leander Rowing Club, Hamilton

My sister Jeannie was still a youngster. They met at Muskoka Lodge. He noticed her the first day and tipped the maître d' for a seat at her table.

When I was an infant, our Walmer Street home was broken into while my sister and I slept. Mom heard the intruder but nervously kept ironing, hoping he wanted to steal something (they hadn't much) and wasn't after the girls. Luckily her hunch proved true.

In 1950, when I was a tiny baby, my mother needed transfusions for an operation that kept her in hospital for six months. Al and his buddies donated blood. Dad was working nights, so I was sent to my grandparents, Meyer and Mira Florence, and their protective dog, Blackie. After that experience, our family, largely apolitical, became supporters of the universal blood bank and national health care.

Dad worked briefly in a shoe store and then in advertising for the Midtown, Biltmore, and other Twentieth Century theatres. He was impressed when the projectionists unionized to improve their pay and working conditions. I recall, as a little girl, trying to no avail to persuade them to stop playing horror movies and triple-bill thrillers.

My dad holding me, aged fourteen months, with my mom in the foreground, at St. John's Convalescent Hospital, Toronto, 1950

Three of the five Perelgut brothers with their parents (left to right: Joe Perell, Harry Perell, Rebecca and Saul Perelgut, Al Perly. Missing are Morris and Phillip)

For years, aside from a mortgage, my parents had no debts. Children of the Depression, they saved to buy things (a car, appliances), never owned credit cards, and believed interest was something good to earn but not to pay. Al eventually started his own businesses, first health clubs and then, with Hannah, a travel agency, which they owned for years. They were all successful enterprises, and he was forced to develop a credit rating. Daddy loved being his own boss and was tolerant of mistakes if promptly confessed and quickly handled. He especially enjoyed planning trips to Israel and honeymoons – often accurately predicting a marriage's longevity based on negotiations in his office. He hated sending clients to Cleveland for coronary bypasses (then the major centre), because some, tragically, never returned.

Mom often joked about her "five years' European experience" and ribbed Al about her being his "war bride." She in turn was teased about her mixed marriage – Litvak to Pole. Hannah was born in the small town of Zidikai, Lithuania, a community of three hundred Jewish families at the turn of the century. Today there are no clues that Jews ever lived there, except for a cemetery a few fields away. There is the well my mother remembered at the main crossroads, and a small museum to commemorate a famous Russian poet born

My maternal grandparents, Meyer and Mira Florence, with their first child, Harold, in Zidikai, Lithuania

there. The Florences kept horse stables in Zidikai. An aged postmistress I met on a teary visit in the late 1980s remembered both families. The Lantins (my grandmother Mira's family) owned a dry-goods store. It was run by Ita, my great-grandmother, who was widowed early, and after whom I am named.

Mira recalled friendly German soldiers during World War I. It is disputed in the family whether a romantic exchange of locks of hair and a bit of jewellery took place between one of the soldiers and my own grandmother or one of her girlfriends. On one occasion, young Mira was forbidden by her parents to attend a speech by the fiery Zionist Jabotinsky. She sneaked out a window and went anyway with her big brother, Efraim. It didn't seem to affect her much; in the forty years I knew her, she was the epitome of moderation, goodness, and reasonable thinking. Once, we kids asked if she was truly Orthodox. She replied, "We're observant but we aren't *meshugge* [crazy]."

A sister, Toby, died young, in 1928. Brother Alex joined my grandparents in Peterborough. Mira received a letter early in 1940, before the Nazi invasion, saying that her mother had died of natural causes. Efraim was perhaps more motivated to "make Aliyah," but he waited too long; he was shot by a German soldier in 1942 while attempting to escape on his bicycle. He had planned to join a girlfriend in Palestine.

During the Russian Revolution, Mira was sent to school near the Black Sea. When the turbulence subsided, she took a well-remembered family train trip to Moscow to visit the sights of the big city. Meyer and Mira married in 1920. Three children were born over the next seven years: Harold, Hannah, and Ruth. Meyer's family generously sent the expectant couple to Memel for their first delivery. Harold arrived in a real hospital with a doctor's assistance. They stayed for two days more in a hotel as an extra treat. Hannah and Ruth were delivered by midwives. Meyer left for Peterborough, Ontario, in 1927 to create a better and safer life for his young family.

Meyer lived with his sister Zelda and brother-in-law Louis. He found a job at de Lavalle, a dairy equipment factory. In 1928 he sent for Mira and the three kids. They went by train from Zidikai to Hamburg, by ship to Halifax and train to Port Hope. Meyer waited at the station in a borrowed truck. Mira and the kids, all fast asleep, almost missed their stop, but fortunately Meyer insisted on boarding the train and found them. Shaking and hugging them, he repeated, "Wake up, wake up" in Yiddish. Impatient employees shuffled them off.

Louis and Zelda (who we called Jenny) had six children, so Mira, Meyer, and their growing family moved into a house on Aylmer Street. Meyer started a business with two friends, Frank and Jake Katz, who were among the "meals only" boarders my grandmother fed. She also offered kosher meals to Jewish soldiers from a nearby army base. The new business involved buying chickens and eggs at local farms and delivering them to Toronto Packing on Spadina Avenue and a similar firm in Montreal. Summer and winter they made the drive, returning with kosher salamis and other treats. Zaidy brought us farm-fresh eggs regularly. The delicious chickens my mom cooked every Friday were, I now realise, far better than most available today. In the early years, if the weather was bad Zaidy slept in the truck. He liked driving and continued to do so well into his seventies. At one time, he owned a Parisienne convertible, a gift from his "son, the doctor" Ralph. Zaidy kept it spotless, and preferred to walk considerable distances rather than take such a precious vehicle outside in snow or rain.

My mother, Hannah Florence, with three of her four brothers and sisters (left to right: Hannah, Harold, and Ruth, with Ralph, seated)

A big fuss was made when Ralph was born, their first child in Canada, followed by Shirley two years later. The kids all went to Prince of Wales Public School and Peterborough Collegiate. They learned to skate (my mom was a terrific skater), to swim, in Chemong Lake, and spoke both English and Yiddish fluently. The boys played hockey, using magazines for knee pads. A potato, cut down the middle, made two viable pucks.

My grandparents loved watermelon (a delicacy, as was all fresh fruit), jello (an amazing new invention), and butter, which they spread thickly on dark Russian bread. They refused corn; "animal feed" they called it. My bubby never wore slacks, always a dress or skirt, to "be a lady." Her cooking was, of course, in the "a little of this, a little of that" style. She laughed at the scientific pretension of today's ridiculously precise recipes. She said, "You just know when it feels right." Her perogen, soups, nothings, matzoh balls, roast chicken, kugels, etc., always felt absolutely right to my many cousins and to me. I only wish we could duplicate them. Everyone believes their bubby was a wonderful cook, but mine really was. She was chosen to teach cooking and home economics at a local school. Zaidy made red wine, which the adults raved about and enjoyed in liberal quantities at dinners and Passover. After my grandfather died, when I was in university, I entered a rare remaining bottle in a campus contest to see how good it really was. It won first prize in the madeira class!

Mira Florence with her five children (left to right: Shirley, Ralph, Ruth, Mira, Harold, and Hannah)

With my husband, Bob Rae, and our daughters, Judith (centre rear), Eleanor, and Lisa (centre front)

Ralph as a young boy once broke *kashrut* by eating forbidden but delicious hot dogs at a picnic. He felt guilty and confessed to his parents. They neither berated nor punished him, saying the decision was his. Ralph went upstairs and promptly threw up.

Harold, the eldest boy, went into business. Hannah and Ruth took commercial courses. My future mom was in her twenties, working as a secretary for General Electric in Toronto, when she met my dad that summer weekend in Muskoka. They dated while she boarded with a family on Palmerston Avenue. As the oldest sister, Hannah took an enormous interest in her brothers and sisters. Shirley lived with us for a few years when I was a toddler.

Ralph was the first to attend university. (Only one brother on my father's side, Joe, got any post-secondary education. This was because of the expense. It was a matter of great pride that in the next generation, so many of us went on to earn degrees.) Ralph worked for years, both before and during his time at medical school, to pay tuition. As a youngster he saved quarters from *shul* errands, such as delivering *lulavs* and *etrogs* to various homes. One of his later jobs consisted of lugging around huge slabs of meat. During med. school he boarded and took meals with his proud and encouraging brother and sisters.

Mira was active in Hadassah (she and my mother were life members), and at the *shul*, helping to settle new arrivals. The family moved to Homewood Avenue, and later to the house I remember on Thompson Avenue, all in

Peterborough. They got along well with their neighbours. A baby carriage was one memorable gift from a gentile family. They frequently visited each other's homes. My bubby's philosophy was simple: "If you're nice to someone, they'll be nice to you."

My earliest memories of Bubby and Zaidy involve driving to Peterborough for weekend visits. Bubby, in apron and housedress, is waiting at the window. Zaidy is in his chair, reading the tiny print of the Yiddish newspaper. The house is noisy, full of food ("have some more"), talk, visitors, squeezed cheeks, and games with familiar objects — a set of pewter coasters, the fluffy comforter on my grandparents' bed. I always wanted the yellow bedroom, but loved the African violet collection in the guest room.

Well into her eighties, living in a seniors' building in Toronto, Bubby volunteered at Baycrest, reading newspapers in Russian or Yiddish to "the old people." She was gentle and undemanding in her own old age, and passed away, the last of my four grandparents and of that remarkable, courageous, and hardworking first generation, in September, 1990.

*I'm on the right in this family
group. On the left is my younger
brother Archie, who was killed
in a motor accident in 1923.*

BEN KAYFETZ

Growing Up on Dundas Street

My earliest recollection goes back to the very early 1920s, sitting on the stoop of our dry-goods store on Spadina Avenue and Baldwin Street (southeast corner), watching the Sunday evening church parade go by. These were the strollers emerging from two nearby Christian churches, the Western Congregational Church, just to the south, and the Christadephian Church on Cecil Street, just to the north. Within a year the scene had radically changed: the two churches had been transformed into synagogues – totally Judaized – the former becoming the Londoner Shul (officially the Men of England), and the latter becoming the Ostrovtzer Shul. The change was symptomatic of two trends: the demographic move of the indigenous Anglo-Saxons out of the Spadina Avenue area, and the trend to Church Union, which reduced the number of Protestant conventicles and effectively removed from the Canadian scene such historic names as Congregationalist, Wesleyan, and Methodist.

Forty years later, when I was employed by the Canadian Jewish Congress, that same dry-goods store was the editorial office of the *Vochenblatt*, a pro-Communist organ of the Left, edited by the late Joshua Gershman. Mr. Gershman maintained a love-hate relationship with me, denouncing me in his paper one week, then beckoning me into his den to present me with the gift of

My mother (centre) and friends in gypsy costume, in Sosnytsya, Ukraine, c. 1906

This Russian-style dandy is my mother's younger brother, David, in Sosnytsya, Ukraine, c. 1910

a book of memoirs by a Yiddish stalwart. His backhanded way of paying a compliment once led him to compare me with another of his targets, fur worker unionist Max Federman. After listing the misdeeds of Federman, the lackey of the capitalist class, he wrote, "But there is one who is even lower than Federman!" And that villainous person was none other than Ben Kayfetz!

Why the dry-goods store? In the year 1918, my father was stricken with a progressive ailment that removed his motor ability, and my mother looked to the store and other livelihoods to care for her family of five children. The two words "dry goods" are to be pronounced *drhygutz*, with a guttural *r*, as it was not until many years later that I learned that this was something other than an accepted Yiddish name for a retail business that dealt in children's clothing.

Within a year we had moved away from Spadina to 893 Dundas Street West, in the Claremont/Bellwoods area, where the house was provided with a storefront that served over the years as a grocery, barbershop, bakery, and finally poultry shop. Some of these enterprises were operated by our family, others by lessees or tenants. Between 1926 and 1929, we leased the property to a barber (who, like many Jewish barbers, doubled as a *klezmer*), and we dwelt at other addresses, never very far away. This area lacked the glamour and colour of Kensington (where we lived briefly in 1926) and had no neighbourhood name to attract interviews by newspaper reporters. It was on the edge of Italian territory – which then consisted of three lone thoroughfares, Manning Avenue, Claremont, and Bellwoods, extending between College and Dundas streets – infinitely smaller than after the massive Italian influx that came after World War II.

We had a rich variety of experiences growing up in this reputedly drab part of Toronto. I recall the excitement of watching herds of cattle being driven down Claremont Street – not on trucks, but on foot – with yapping dogs running alongside! This was not a one-time only procedure; I remember it happening several times. The incongruity of cattle treading on a paved road in a built-up urban area never occurred to us children. Years later, when I mentioned this in company, I was greeted by total disbelief – so much so that to escape embarrassment I gave up telling the story. But then I found confirmation in the memory of Johnny Lombardo, of Radio CHIN, who is approximately my age and was raised in the same neighbourhood. The only difference is that, in his recollection, the cattle were moving northward. (This is unlikely, because they were probably being driven south to the abattoir at the foot of Tecumseh Street, having started their "walk" at the Junction stockyards.)

I remember one thing from our brief stay in Kensington in 1926. There was a group of boys who had a ongoing handball game on Baldwin Street every weekday. But on Saturday, no game! Under traffic conditions today, such a sport would be unthinkable, but in 1926 it was possible; Sabbath observance reigned supreme. All shops were Jewish and all were shut down. The main shopping day was Thursday in preparation for the Sabbath that came the following Friday evening.

Who were our neighbours on Dundas Street? There was Mr. Baker, the *damski shneider* (ladies' tailor), whose neighbour the cobbler read him the Yiddish daily newspaper. In the tradition of *heymishe shneiders*, he was Jewishly illiterate. Then there was Richman, the *shuster*, who carried on in turn in three stores all within one block and whose billboard proclaimed he had cobbled shoes in all the capitals of Europe! The modest, learned parents of Dr. Ben Cohen, staunch General Zionists, lived in the neighbourhood. Another family were shnapps dealers, the polite word for bootleggers. They moved, appropriately, to Chicago, but when they moved back to Toronto three years later they had graduated to South Parkdale.

I made mention of the Londoner Shul, which boasted an imperial connection. But the members were hardly true-blue, hearts-of-oak Englishmen as one might think from the name. My Uncle Paysha was a member, and goodness knows there was little that was English about him. Whence the Anglophile title? It dawned on me years later. It was the practice at the turn of the century for immigrant ships to stop at an English port such as Liverpool for quarantine purposes. The stay lasted about two weeks, just long enough for the Litvak immigrants to acquire a taste of tweed tailoring, a pipe, and the other paraphernalia of civilized British living. And they proposed to continue this pretence as a touch of Old England. Years later they made an unsuccessful attempt to affiliate with the Board of Deputies of British Jews in Britain.

Another *shul* – much humbler in its structure, occupying a *shtiebl* on lower Huron Street – bore the pretentious, "big-city" name of the Anshe New York. Most *landsmanshaftn* were named for Eastern European *shtetlekh* or provinces. But New York? hardly a name to conjure up shtetl memories! Years later I found the answer. These were a group of needle workers who worked together and prayed together. Dependent on the seasonal supply of work in Toronto and

My uncle David and his bride, Reveka. He died young, in 1912, possibly due to injuries he inflicted on himself in an attempt to avoid Tsarist army service.

Top: Four of the five Kayfetz children with their mother. I am on the right.

Bottom: A class photo at Manning Avenue School, June 1925. Eight-year-old Ben Kayfetz is seated in the second row, fourth from the right. The man with the white beard was the principal, Charles G. Fraser, after whom the school was later named. Because he often wore a black skull-cap, the rumour arose that he must have had a Jewish ancestor.

June 1925

My maternal grandparents, Hillel and Basya Orloff, in Toronto, c. 1927. Hillel put on a sheitel (wig) over her white hair for this photograph, making herself unrecognizable.

New York, they moved from one location to the other when the season changed. But in the mid-1920s, the United States lowered the boom on immigration. There was no longer an open border, and the group found themselves confined to Canada's soil. So they remained in Toronto, stayed in the needle trade, and continued worshipping together as Anshe New York in memory of the "open border"!

Nineteen twenty-seven marked the tenth anniversary of the Russian Revolutions. I use the plural, for as we know there were two: the February and the October. I, like the Revolution, was ten years old. My mother, I'm sure,

In this photo, taken in the 1930s, are my mother's kinfolk left behind in Soviet Russia. Her oldest sister, Chaya (centre), lost all but one of her six or eight children in the pogroms of the early 1920s. From the left are Chaya's husband, her one surviving daughter, and her son-in-law. Contact with the family was lost in 1939.

was unaware of the distinction between the two political upheavals. She knew there had been a revolution which was long desired by the oppressed people of Russia (she had left in 1907), and in a vague way she favoured anything that removed the hated hand of Tsarism and pogroms. She still recalled with favour words like "democracy" and "Duma." Which is why I found myself seated with her at a public meeting in the Ukrainian Labour Temple on Bathurst Street (opposite Alexandra Park). There were lengthy speeches in Ukrainian, of which I understood not a word. What I do recall is a speech in English, heavily accented by the Glaswegian dialect thereof, by a top Communist party official named Jock MacDonald, who had praise and homage for the Bolshevik Revolution. What marred his speech, however, were the gales of laughter from the audience hearing his praise for the *Rooshan* Revolution and his panegyric for Soviet *Roosha*. And within a year this Scottish proletarian was in disgrace, no longer secretary general of the party. He had made the wrong choice politically, having opted for the Trotskyist faction. This was my first lesson in dialectical materialism and the impermanence of political correctness.

My first experience in a mushroom synagogue was early in the 1920s, when I attended such a service in the Templars' Hall on Queen Street West, just beside the 999 Queen Street Insane Asylum as we so insensitively called it. An uncle of ours had a hardware business on Queen Street West (which duly failed). With other Jewish shopkeepers they hired the Templars' Hall for the High Holidays. I was seated in the gods, perched near the ceiling, and had no good coign of vantage to watch the proceedings. But what I did see was the blessing of the *kohanim* (priests), a procedure which gave me an eerie, fearful feeling. The figures, totally enveloped in *talaysim* (prayer shawls) from head to toe, arms outstretched but completely cloaked, rocking back and forth like automatons to the rhythm of the murmured blessing, resembled huge machines. It came as no surprise to be told that if one looked at them one risked being struck blind!

There was a Mr. Bloom (grandfather of poet Phyllis Gottlieb) — whose fur shop was in the same Queen Street/Dovercourt Road area — for whom mother did "finishing work" at home. A venerable, patriarchal figure (though he was clean shaven), his appearance and age demanded respect and deference. Occasionally he would telephone our home about my mother's fur work, and when my sister answered she spoke in her less-than-perfect Yiddish, as that was how one addressed elderly Jews. He would reply in flawless, unaccented

English. But my sister still addressed him in Yiddish; she knew of no other way of addressing the elderly, even if they were clean shaven.

At one point in the mid-twenties, my mother answered an advertisement in the Yiddish daily looking for a cook general on a Jewish-owned farm near Georgetown. It wasn't clear to her whether this was to be a summer resort, a favourite sideline for Jewish farmers (witness the Catskills). For some reason she took me along for the ride. I was all of nine. We travelled on the old Toronto–Guelph radial line (long since defunct), and I recall passing such exotic-sounding stations as Eldorado Park, and some less exotic names as Streetsville, Cooksville, Erindale. I was not present at the interview, but remember sitting alone in the radial car station awaiting my mother's return. My mother did not accept the job. We returned home and I forgot the episode. More than thirty years later I received a telephone call at the office of the Canadian Jewish Congress from a Mr. Morris Saxe and was asked to come to his daughter's home, where he had some documents to leave with the Congress. I found him in bed (he died within the year), and he proceeded to tell me of his abortive attempt in the 1920s to train and settle on the land up to seventy-five Jewish children living in a orphanage in Mezritch in Eastern Poland. This idealistic plan failed, sabotaged, he said, by politicians and others who had their own agenda. He wanted the documents to be left with a communal agency like the Congress as it was a piece of history that ought to be preserved. (In one respect, the project was a success, saving the seventy-five from Hitler's killers some fifteen years later.)

I spent several hours with Mr. Saxe and accepted the documents. On the way home it occurred to me that Morris Saxe was the prospective employer – the Georgetown dairy farmer – who had interviewed my mother back in the 1920s! Now I recalled what he said about his wife, who in the end had to take on the mammoth task of cooking for and feeding the youngsters – a job which Mr. Saxe said was responsible for her premature death. It was this punishing task that my mother had happily avoided.

More recently Mr. Saxe's grandson, David Fleishman, has made a film entitled *A Man of Conscience* about this almost-forgotten episode in Ontario Jewish history, an episode in which I unwittingly had a very minor role.

When newsboys were not yet extinct: Me at 15 years old, Queen and Roncesvalles, 1932

My parents, in Ostrowiec, Poland, 1918

Early Jewish Doctors and the Health Care of Jewish Immigrants in Toronto

The area of Toronto in which Jewish immigrants first settled was called the Ward. In the later nineteenth century, this area, from College Street south to Gerrard, and Yonge Street west to University Avenue, was really a ward in the true sense. It was a ghetto, shared by immigrant Jews and Irish and Italian Catholics. Later, streets such as McCaul, Henry, and Beverley were regarded as part of the Ward even though they were west of University Avenue. The Jews had come from turn-of-the-century pogroms and persecutions in Romania, Hungary, Poland, and Russia. By 1911 there were more than ten thousand inhabitants in the Ward's 147 acres, and 70 per cent of them were Jews. In some of the streets, such as Chestnut, Elizabeth, Elm, and Edward and adjacent areas, there were nearly 1,400 small, pinched little houses where now there are only about 50 buildings. Russian Jews and Italians lived side by side on Centre Avenue, which was considered desirable because it was near the Harrison Public Baths.

Dr. Samuel Lavine, Toronto's first Jewish doctor, graduated in 1889 from Trinity College, which later became part of the University of Toronto. His office was on the east side of Beverley Street, near Baldwin. He charged fifty cents for a consultation and made his calls on a bicycle, unlike the

My father, Yisroel Weinberg, emigrated from Poland in 1920. As soon as he made a few dollars as a furrier in Toronto, he bought a church and made it into the Ostrovitzer Shul at Cecil and Spadina.

The Ostrovitzer Shul

well-established practitioners who wore high silk hats and made their rounds in fancy horse-drawn carriages. Dr. Solomon Singer, Toronto's second Jewish doctor, started his practice in 1905 at 280 Simcoe Street. His list of patients increased quickly and he was appointed a coroner, but his career was short-lived. He died in 1913 of typhoid fever, which he contracted from a patient.

Until 1910 there were only these two Jewish medical practitioners in Toronto. By that time there were already 18,000 Jewish people in the city, and it is obvious that most Jewish patients were treated by non-Jewish doctors, even in the Jewish sick-benefit lodges. It was natural for the recently arrived Yiddish-speaking immigrants to group themselves into *landsmanshaftn* societies or lodges, which provided sick benefits to their members. The young Jewish doctors had their first contacts in the communities through these lodges. The older, settled, English-speaking members of the Jewish community didn't call on Jewish doctors until some years later.

Between 1908 and 1912 the roster of Jewish medical graduates grew to include five physicians available for the medical care of the Jewish community. Dr. A. I. Willinsky, who graduated in 1908, was in general practice for a time at College and Henry streets, and also for a while at 166 John Street, in quarters provided for him thanks to the help of a friend of the family, the Rev. Maurice Kaplan, the Cantor of the McCaul Street Synagogue. Dr. "A. I.", as he was generally known, recalls that when he looked for post-graduate training in Toronto, he was told: "You would never get anything in Toronto, Willinsky. Give it up here, you will have to go away." And in fact A. I. did go away, and specialized in many fields and studied under men of great skill in many parts of the world. He returned to Toronto and later became the chief of urological surgery at the Western Hospital, on Bathurst Street. Despite an international reputation and attracting patients to the Western from all over the world, he never did get a university teaching appointment in Toronto.

The next group of Jewish physicians included Dr. M. A. Pollock (class of 1911), Dr. L. J. Breslin (1912, and silver medalist in his class), and Drs. Benjamin Cohen, William Harris, David Perlman, and Harry Feader (all members of the class of 1918 and enlisted in the Canadian army during World War I).

After the war, in the four years between 1919 and 1923, twenty-three Jewish doctors started practice, more than tripling the number of Jewish physicians in Toronto. Their offices for the most part were in the Jewish neighbourhood: Dundas Street between McCaul and Bathurst.

These doctors still found it difficult to develop a practice amongst their own people, or even to be elected to the Jewish sick-benefit lodges. The Jewish community had developed a pattern of dependence on non-Jewish doctors, and it took time for the Jewish immigrants to develop confidence in their own and recommend Jewish doctors for positions in their lodges.

During this period Jewish doctors began to meet and form their own medical society. They gathered informally in each other's homes or in the four Jewish-owned drugstores: Hashmalls, Rothbarts, and Mirochnik's, all on Dundas Street West, or Koffler's, on College Street at the corner of Borden. It wasn't until 1921 that they met at the offices of Dr. M. A. Pollock on Bloor Street for the purpose of organizing a more formal Jewish Medical Society. The following year the Mount Sinai, Toronto's first Jewish hospital, was founded and provided a focus for Jewish medical expertise and fellowship.

Before 1922, when the Mount Sinai was established at 100 Yorkville Avenue, there had been a very interesting attempt at providing medical care for Jewish immigrants, especially infants and children. This was the Free Jewish Dispensary, started in 1903, first on Elizabeth Street near Agnes (now Dundas), and later, from January 3, 1912, in a three-storey building at 19 Simcoe Street, the top floor of which was used as a home for Jewish orphans.

This dispensary was a great help for struggling newcomers who spoke only Yiddish. Mrs. Dorothy Dworkin (née Goldstick), who had trained as a maternity nurse, was in charge. Mrs. Ida Siegal (née Lewis) was much involved with the dispensary and with volunteer groups who helped the immigrants.

There were many people associated with the Free Jewish Dispensary. Some names still remembered and respected in the Jewish community are Mr. M. Langbord, Dr. Lyon, Mr. Shulman, two Benjamin brothers, Drs. Singer, Willinsky, and Levine, and Dr. Bessie Pullen, Toronto's first woman Jewish doctor. In 1918, during the devastating flu epidemic, a temporary branch of this dispensary was opened at 81 McCaul Street to provide additional medical care for the Jewish population.

The year 1875 marks the founding of a specialized children's hospital sponsored by the philanthropic McMaster family. The hospital moved a number of times until a permanent site was found in 1892 at 67 College Street at Elizabeth Street and the dream of the founding families of the Hospital for Sick Children had become a reality. A completely new outpatient department was opened in 1915 as part of this new hospital and extended down the east side of Elizabeth.

Entrance to the Hospital for Sick Children outpatient department, c. 1915. The notice in Yiddish reads, "Only the poor . . ."

My uncles and cousin in Poland (note the typical Polish Jewish hat and coat). They were never heard from after the Nazi invasion of Poland.

The new wing and the outpatient department entrance are shown in the above photograph. Of course the sign had to be in Yiddish to be understood by the many Jewish families who came to the hospital for treatment, and was probably also meant to appeal to this immigrant group to make use of the facility, for experience in Eastern Europe had instilled in these people a fear of hospitals. The second-largest group of newcomers who lived in the Ward were from Italy, so one interesting sign inside the hospital, instructing parents to wash out infant feeding bottles before returning them, is in both Yiddish and Italian.

The increase in Jewish immigration to Toronto to over 18,000 by 1911 was due to the Canadian government's encouragement of Jewish immigrants to come over and work on the railway, on farms, and in other areas. In addition, Jews came over to cut forests and to form Jewish communities out west in the prairies.

The significant increase in the Jewish population in those years is also explained by the practice of immigrant men sending for their wives, children, and relatives. Although the economical level of these families was low in Canada, it was better than conditions in Europe. In Toronto they became rag-pickers, butchers, bakers, junk dealers, pedlars selling small wares, as well as fur and clothing factory workers.

Nurses' station, 1915, for the pick-up and return of bottles of pasteurized milk for mothers who couldn't nurse. The signs on the wall, in Yiddish and Italian, ask mothers to please "bring the bottles back clean."

One of the most famous names involved in child care in Toronto, and a particular favourite of Jewish families, was Dr. Alan Brown, who became the Physician-in-Chief of the Hospital for Sick Children. He had a good deal of contact with the leading children's physicians of Europe who were Jewish. There was one paediatrician who had a great influence on Brown – Professor Heinrich Finkelstein of Berlin, who had by then published an authoritative text on diseases of infants. It was from Finkelstein that Brown learned the use of acidified milks in the treatment of intestinal disease, a diarrhea scourge that was the major child-killer on the wards of the old hospital in the pre-Alan Brown era. And in Alan Brown's postgraduate work he had been influenced by the teachings of the famous Dr. Abraham Jacobi, a Jewish ex-patriot paediatrician who fostered the first teaching clinics for children in America and is considered the father of American paediatrics. Brown taught generations of medical students in the style that he learned from Finkelstein and Jacobi and became the first to specialize in child care.

The Jewish influence on Alan Brown went further. While he was studying in New York he had moved in fashionable social circles where he had observed great Jewish philanthropists at work for the welfare of poor children. One of these was Nathan Straus, the founder of the New York City Milk Fund for poor children. The Straus brothers, owners of Macy's department store, strongly supported many child welfare causes. These were the German Jews of the "Our Crowd" – aristocracy who accepted great social consciousness as a responsibility of their wealth. Brown seems to have followed these models by his efforts to interest the Toronto business elite in similar causes.

Over the years, as the Jewish community grew farther north in Toronto and became more integrated into the medical and scientific community, the little Jewish hospital on Yorkville Avenue grew and developed into the Mount Sinai Hospital on University Avenue, a world-renowned centre for medical care and research, not just of the Jewish community, but still focused on the new immigrant communities of Asians, Italians, and Portuguese. And of course, Jewish doctors now gained entry into all the hospitals of Toronto, and indeed were often leading physicians in those facilities.

How I Got My First Bicycle

At 5 years old, with my mother, Ruchel

It was during the Depression years and we lived on Grace Street near College and the kid up the street got a shiny new two-wheel bicycle for his Bar Mitzvah. I had my Bar Mitzvah at about the same time, and what did I get? Books and pyjamas. And just what did I really want? A shiny new two-wheeler like he had.

We were not poor, but in those days my parents did not feel that getting me a bicycle was so important. I did eventually get one, however, but thereby hangs a tale.

Mr. Isaacson, who owned a drugstore on the corner of Grace and College, had the idea that whoever made the most purchases in a three-month period would get the shiny blue bicycle that hung so wondrously in the window of his store. He also installed a huge thermometer in the window, and

The Standard Fur Co., 317 Adelaide Street, in the 1930s. The company made fur collars and cuffs for the clothing trade. My father, the handsome suited figure, was the outside man, the fur buyer.

each day the names of the contestants and the value of their purchases would climb the scale, simulating rising temperature.

The big bicycle store in the Jewish district in those days was Himel's on Dundas Street, and on a Sunday Jewish radio program there was a jingle which encouraged people to *"koyfts bei Himel."*

Well, I got my whole family involved, uncles, aunts, friends, distant relatives, all of whom made their purchases at Isaacson's for whatever — toothpaste, Band-Aids, iodine, Odorono deodorant, etc., and they would give me the receipts to be added to my total score.

Despite all my efforts and those of my family, I was forever second from the top, always out-purchased by the son of Mr. Widman, whose barbershop was a few doors along from Isaacson's on the south side of College Street. Anybody who had a haircut at Widman's was asked to contribute receipts for his son.

As the contest was closing, it was nip and tuck between the Widman offspring and myself, until a scheme initiated by my father put me in the running. In those days all male adults that I knew smoked cigarettes, and my dad would purchase his from a Mr. Naiman, who moonlighted selling Player's Navy Cut, which he delivered in a brown paper bag every few weeks. At the last moment before the contest ended, my dad went into Isaacson's drugstore and purchased a huge amount of cigarettes, indeed his whole stock, which he immediately sold to Mr. Naiman. In that way my dad got his money back and I had a huge receipt to submit at the last minute of the last day of the contest. And that's how I got a shiny new blue two-wheeler bicycle for my Bar Mitzvah.

My daughter Sari had a bike very much like mine, but she didn't have to win a contest. She was a good kid, so we bought it for her eighth birthday. How times have changed.

My mother and father

EDWIN GOODMAN

Many Are Our Joys

The grey horse and wagon with the diminutive muscular man and his young son sitting up front had just passed through the gates of the Halton County farm. The equipage was immediately surrounded by running children calling out to their mother, "Here comes the Jew, here comes the Jew." This was my father's earliest memory. It was the mid-eighteen nineties and he was a three- or four-year-old child accompanying his dad as he carted his wares of clothing and pots and pans and other bric-a-brac from farm to farm in Halton and Peel counties. A few years later the family moved from Acton, Ontario, to Wingham, where my grandfather continued to earn his livelihood in this fashion. While he didn't start a commercial dynasty like Timothy Eaton, he did well enough to move to Toronto, where he bought a house on Centre Avenue, now the site of an addition to the Toronto General Hospital. There he completed his family of four boys and three girls; my father was the second child and eldest son.

Today, as I look back from the perspective of seventy years, the scenes of my memory shift and change; faces and places of my youth flash by, coming in and out of focus like images in a kaleidoscope. I see my family in the foreground, my mother always beautiful at every age, and my younger sister, still

At age 3 or 4, in typical attire

lovely today, my father coming home from his law office as my sister and I dashed for the paper to spread on the living-room floor of our house on Palmerston Boulevard. My paternal grandparents sitting in the kitchen of their home on Lennox Street playing gin rummy, my grandmother catching my grandfather cheating.

I see my grandfather as a short, tough, bad-tempered man and my grandmother as a beautiful quiet woman – and the only person alive who could handle my irascible grandfather. Charles Goodman came to Canada in 1881 from the part of Galicia that is now Moravia in Czechoslovakia. He arrived at the age of eleven totally alone and unable to speak English. He was the courageous forerunner of the rest of his family, who were to follow shortly once he had reconnoitred the scene and earned a little money to help them settle here.

Fifty years after my father's family had moved to Toronto from Wingham I had a drink with Jack Hanna, the elderly member of the provincial Legislature for Huron County, which included Wingham. I said to him, "My grandfather lived in Wingham and two of my uncles were born there around the turn of the century."

"Was your grandfather Charles Goodman?" he asked, and I nodded. "Charlie the Jew," he mused, "was the toughest guy that ever came to Wingham. I remember him well. He had to be tough to be the only Jew in Wingham and survive."

Stern and tough though he was, it was not Charles Goodman who made an imprint on his children, it was his wife, Sarah. Every one of the four sons took a second name beginning with B as homage to her maiden name of Brody. Nor did Charles's orthodox religious outlook and his dedication to the synagogue take hold with any of his children. It was their mother's commitment to the cause of a Jewish national homeland through Hadassah-wizo that shaped their contribution to the Jewish community.

The romance of my parents' marriage always intrigued me. They met at a skating rink, and my dad pursued the auburn beauty from when she was sixteen until he finally captured her at age twenty-one. His chief allies were lilies-of-the-valley and roses and gifts of candy, which he continued to lavish on her until his death, bringing home two pounds of Laura Secord chocolates every Friday night. (I was well into adolescence before I learned that our family's habit of biting into a chocolate and leaving the bitten half for someone else wasn't acceptable social behaviour.)

*My father, D. B. Goodman, assumes
presidency of the Habonim, an early
Zionist organization, in the early 1920s*

In September 1917, my parents eloped and were married in Hamilton.
They then each returned to their separate homes, telling no one of the wedding. Just why, neither ever explained to me. Unfortunately for their plans of
secrecy, a Jewish wedding requires a *minyon*, a quorum of ten men. One of the
men they had called in knew my maternal grandfather and telephoned him the
next day with the news. My mother then joined her new husband in my grandfather's house on Brunswick Avenue until they were able to buy a house on
Indian Road Crescent near High Park in Toronto. I was born there in October
1918 during the great influenza epidemic.

When I shake my memory kaleidoscope it is my mother's image that
appears most often. She was a chestnut-haired, blue-eyed, petite beauty whose
grandparents came to Canada from Russia via the U.S.A. about the same time
as my father's family. She was in charge of my education, both formal and
informal, and fortunately for me she was an incurable romantic.

Even in my name my mother's love of romantic history shows. She called
me Edwin instead of Elliott, which was closer to my Hebrew name, Elia.
Edwin was the name of the king of Northumbria in England in the seventh
century about whom my mother had read in one of her much-loved historical
novels. Edwin I was the first Northumbrian king to convert to Christianity, an
act that so enraged his subjects that they destroyed his heathen temple at
Goodmanham. The connection was too much for my mother to resist.

My father (right) and his three brothers, Louis, Max, and Sam

My own first recollection, at the age of three, is of the house on Palmerston Boulevard into which we moved in 1921. Palmerston was a broad boulevard lined with huge trees and elegant gaslight standards whose white globes lent an air of magic to the solid brick houses and the solid burghers who lived there. Garfield Weston and his family lived a few blocks north of our house, and our block boasted the residence of Sam McBride, the future mayor of Toronto. To my mother's consternation, on the very first day, not five minutes into the house, I pedalled my fire engine into a lamp.

We continued to live on Palmerston Boulevard until just after the outbreak of war in 1939. My mother had a quiet confidence that our family was different and that her children should be outfitted to reflect their special status. At three and four I was wearing Eton suits with hard collars and beautiful reefer coats. At six, I was at Clinton Street Public School sporting the only tie in the entire class. Class picture after class picture shows that Goodman alone had a necktie. Goodman alone had to wear shorts and then breeches, never long pants. Not until I was in high school and found myself to be the only person at Harbord Collegiate sporting breeches did I rise in righteous indignation and persuade my mother to buy me long pants.

My enrolment at Harbord was the result of a victory against my mother's well-meaning plans for her only son. She had me entered and accepted at Upper Canada College, but I prevailed on her to let me go with my friends to Harbord, which in those days held the joint records of graduating the most scholarship students in Ontario while expelling more pupils per capita than any other school in the province.

The advantages of my mother's sensitivity, however, far outweighed the momentary embarrassments she caused me. From the age of five I went to the theatre every week. The Ballets Russes de Monte Carlo never came to Toronto without my being privileged to see it. Long before I was old enough to walk alone to the children's public library on St. George Street, my mother would tramp with me through the snow to take out books. To this day my own library sports dozens of old volumes of the Bobbsey Twins series and *Bunnie Brown and His Sister Sue* with the dated inscriptions, "To Edwin from Mother with love – 1925." How fortunate I was to have been born before the age of television and to parents who regularly spent the evenings reading. Our house was always filled with books, and it seems to me that much of what I know today dates back to what I read in my childhood and youth.

With fellow officers in England before the invasion (I am second from the left)

In furtherance of my mother's cultural educational program, I used to have to take my sister – then called Cecelé, now Cecily, and one of the loveliest brightest women in Toronto – who was six years my junior, to her ballet lessons at The Boris Volkoff School of ballet. It is my belief that whatever contribution I made to the formation and early survival of the National Ballet of Canada can be traced to those hours I waited around the Volkoff studio wishing fervently that I could have been playing football.

My mother's early disappointment was her failure to make me a concert pianist. A stream of excellent teachers tried pleading, threatening, and in one case even beating my hands to a pulp, to no avail. I would practise my scales desultorily while reading a book. I would push the clock ahead so that I could persuade myself that I wasn't lying about my practice time. My ear for music and for languages has always been of the purest tin.

When I entered public school, my parents were convinced that they had reared a prodigy. Before I started school, they had already taught me to read and write and to recite poetry. My mother was confident that all she had to do was take me to the schoolhouse door and I would be revealed to the world. For the first three years they were right. Thanks largely to their efforts, I was educated far beyond any of my classmates. I received my come-uppance relatively quickly, however. When I was in Senior Second, or Grade 4, a new boy named

Walter Edick arrived in the class. Up until that time, I could add faster than anybody, was far better read, and had no problem with my examinations. Imagine my chagrin when I found that Edick could add faster than I could. He went on to trounce me soundly in the examinations, and it was all downhill from there. Apart from achieving a good standing in graduate law school, I was never much of a scholar. Walter taught me one of my most valuable lessons — that there were a lot of people around who were cleverer than I was. I would just have to get along in the world by working harder than the next guy.

I joined the 60th Wolf Cub Pack at the age of seven. It was the beginning of a wonderful association, lasting for more than ten years, with the Boy Scout movement, and today I am proud to be the Honorary President of the Boy Scouts of Canada, Greater Toronto Region. Scouting taught me the importance of such basic values in life as a love of nature, self-reliance, and a sense of community. Much of my pride in being a Canadian and enjoying the great wilderness country comes from the Scout movement.

I was bitten by the political bug just before the onset of puberty, whence I date my other youthful interest — women. But for this accident of chronology, I might never have found politics. In 1930 the country was in the beginning of the Depression, when William Lyon Mackenzie King, the prime minister and leader of the Liberal Party, called an election. My father had articled and spent the first years of his practice as a junior to E.W.J. Owens, a lawyer and Conservative member of the Ontario Legislative Assembly for Toronto Centre West, a part of the city not too far from where we lived. This association had brought many people in public life to our house, including G. Reginald Geary, the former mayor of Toronto, then the federal Member of Parliament for Trinity riding. My dad, though only in his mid-thirties, was Geary's official agent, and as such was responsible for the expenditures made on Geary's campaign.

Joe Eisenberg, then a cigar maker, later a printer, and forever an inveterate cigar smoker (you might say almost an eater), was a friend of my parents and used to drop around to our house. Joe's heavy-jowled and broad-featured face with its cigar protruding would later become well known to thousands of Tories across the whole province. He was one of the party's most ardent workers both federally and provincially. When I ran for the Legislature fifteen years later he was still at my side. For immigrants who had fled Europe, the world "liberal" stood for tolerance, the word "conservative" for oppression. In 1930

Eisenberg was a member of a small group of Jews who were Conservatives. The vast majority were Liberals and remain so today. I was eleven when Joe took me out and gave me my first course in politics. I was to deliver signs up and down College, Clinton, and Manning streets for Colonel Geary. The election focused sharply on the two leaders. King had been Liberal leader since 1919, after he returned to Canada from the United States. The Conservative leader since 1927 was Richard Bedford Bennett, a Calgary lawyer. King was a shrewd, wily bachelor who believed in the spirit world. Bennett was a forceful, abrasive, strong-willed, and stubborn man who believed in reality. Except for a few months in 1926, King had been prime minister since 1921, but the world economic depression made the outcome of the 1930 election so hard to predict that an eleven-year-old had as good a chance of being right as anyone.

I had just come home from one of my signposting forays, during which I had been exposed to the predominantly Liberal sentiments of the Italian and Jewish storekeepers. Fortunately in those days the area still had a strong Anglo-Saxon contingent that was more receptive to my Conservative importuning. Puzzled by the hostility I had encountered, I turned to my father and asked ingenuously, "Why are we Conservatives?"

My dad thought for a moment, then replied, "I guess it's because I have always found them more decent." In retrospect it was not an answer I would have expected from a tolerant, objective man like my father, but I accepted it then without question and it remained in my mind. Since then, I have tried to use decency as the yardstick by which I measure politicians. I also admire people of moderation like my father, and decency and moderation often go hand in hand.

The Tories won the election, and Reginald Geary won in Trinity, going on to become Minister of Justice. I had backed a winner and in one stroke I was turned into a life-long addict of politics. It would have been hard for Colonel Geary to lose. Toronto in the early thirties had little demographic resemblance to Toronto today, even in its central core. The city was British in population and outlook and, except for a lively Irish community, overwhelmingly Protestant and Orange – and Orange meant Tory. The Orange Order delivered every Toronto seat but one to Bennett in 1930. Sam Factor won a lone victory in Toronto West Centre (later Spadina) riding for the Liberals.

My precocious interest in politics was nurtured by the annual municipal elections. Aspiring candidates sought the benefit of my father's advice, assistance, and prestige. He often helped in getting out the voters on election days

Top: With my two daughters, Diane (right) and Joanne (left), skiing in Switzerland

Bottom: Sue and Edwin Goodman with Kathy and Bill Davis in Israel in the eighties

Top: Diane Goodman being presented to Her Majesty Queen Elizabeth II at the Royal Ontario Museum, September 1983, with her mother, Sue (extreme right), looking on

Bottom: At the Royal Ontario Museum, 1986

and I was soon familiar with many aldermanic committee rooms. There I was attracted by the excitement — and by the corned-beef sandwiches, another of my many enduring weaknesses.

Like most people starting to grow old, my memories of my youth appear clear and colourful while I have some difficulty remembering what I had for lunch today. Our family was close, loving, and happy. My early environment was largely Jewish but was influenced more by my parents' Zionist proclivities than by specifically religious concerns. My mother and my father were active in furthering the dream of Theodor Herzl, the intellectual and spiritual founder of the movement for the establishment of a Jewish national homeland in Palestine. At twelve I joined Young Judaea, a youth component of the movement. My sister Cecily did far more for the Zionist dream than I have. I remained an active Zionist, but she became president of Canadian Hadassah-WIZO after numerous positions on the ladder.

I attended Holy Blossom Temple Sunday school from the age of seven. It was a reformed or, if you'll pardon the expression, "liberal" synagogue. It also had the historic honour of being the first synagogue established in Toronto. Originally an orthodox synagogue on Richmond Street where my grandparents on both sides were members, it later moved to Bond Street, and from there to Bathurst Street near Eglinton, where it stands today.

In the early thirties, Holy Blossom did not give young men a Bar Mitzvah ceremony; they had a later confirmation. I was bar mitzvahed at my grandfather's *shul* (synagogue) on Markham Street, which he and his cronies and grandsons had helped renovate with their own labour. He had gone there when he was ousted as president of the large Galician synagogue on Bay Street, where the Eaton Centre now stands. Despite the months of hard work by my private tutor, I stumbled over the ancient Hebrew words when I read from the scrolls of the Torah. Years later, my two daughters did much better.

My close relationship with my parents made me the recipient of everything that a boy could want — except a bicycle, which my mother felt was too dangerous. I may be the only child ever who received boxing gloves at the age of nine or ten and was encouraged to get knocked out by his older friends, but was denied a bicycle. I got even with mother, however. I now have three bicycles and I ride them everywhere, in traffic whose density was never dreamt of in the 1930s.

PART TWO

TROUBLE IN THE GOLDENA MEDINA

Beatrice Shapiro in middy-blouse
(Haybull Studio, Woodstock)

BEATRICE FISCHER

Growing Up in Woodstock

When my siblings and I were growing up in Woodstock, Ontario, we were too involved in our adolescent angst to solicit and record our parents' history. Now we are grown and look back with longing, the history is gone from us. But when I was offered this assignment to record what it was like to grow up Jewish, I began to unearth the old sepia photos. I phoned my sisters in New York and Florida to pump them, and I read them what I had written up to that point. . . . No, no. You have it all wrong! Mama was not born in Bobruisk, it was Minsk. Mama came by boat in 1910, not 1914. Her name was Friedman, no it was Walenschik, it was changed at Ellis Island. Mama and Daddy met at a dance in Brooklyn. No, they met at a bus stop in New York. They courted two years, or was it seven . . .

No matter. Our parents' mark remains indelibly imprinted on us four survivors. My mother's face is reflected in my granddaughter Zaza's face. My father's take on the English language enriches all our exchanges. During a particularly tense pinochle game, Daddy once exhorted Mr. Shecter of Ingersoll, Mr. Brown of Guelph, and Mr. Gerofsky of Stratford: "Gentlemens, I'm independing on you!"

Me and Mama in front of the railway station in Woodstock, early 1920s

My beloved mother, Fanny Friedman, and her father. She had paid for his fare to New York.

Well, it was Zakalnov, and Mama was one of eleven children, nine by her parents and two adopted, as was the custom, after a cousin died. Mama was clever; she taught Russian to Russian children. She carried her shoes and her books to school and had dreams of an intellectual life. But instead she had to prepare herself to emigrate to the United States, because her father, a poor rabbi, could not make a living in Zakalnov. Mama was seventeen, the age of my first-born granddaughter. She was to get a job, find a place to live, and then my grandfather would join her. My bubby packed sandwiches, a salami, and Mama's favourite book, *Twenty Thousand Leagues Under the Sea,* and Mama set off. The year was 1909, I think. I know the weather turned rotten. Mama was by then on the boat, hundreds of immigrants heaving on the lowest decks. Only beer could keep my mother from seasickness, so she established a nice little business on the stairways to the upper decks, exchanging salami slices for beer, and made a little profit as well.

Armed with photographs, letters, and addresses of relatives who had already arrived in New York, Mama found a place to live and a job in a shirt-waist factory. She lived even more frugally than her circumstances required, and put away every penny to bring her father to New York. Meanwhile, she met, courted, and married my father, who had emigrated from Bobruisk to New York, spurred on by a hostile stepmother. Oh, the holes in the narrative! Did my grandfather return brokenhearted to Zakalnov because he couldn't find a place for himself in the maelstrom of the lower East Side in New York? A relative mentioned to me that he had a pushcart, but I don't believe it. It would have been beneath his dignity.

My sister was born in 1915, while a giant flu epidemic raged in New York. Desperate, my father gathered up my mother and sister and took a night train to Buffalo. Aunt Udysse already lived in Toronto, so they came here, and Daddy got a job at Tip Top Tailors. They lived near Aunt Udysse on Kensington (or was it Baldwin?). Meanwhile, Daddy dreamt of independence and a little *gescheft*. One day, while walking on Spadina Avenue, he miraculously bumped into a cousin, Harry Shapiro, from Stratford. They talked, then determined to make sure they would not be separated by more than thirty miles. And so my father moved to Woodstock. He had no prospects, but he did have a wife whom he adored and, by then, two daughters. He found a little apartment over the Chinese laundry. (Or was it at 21 Dover Street, which I do indeed remember? In fact we have all been back many times to photograph, to recall, to laugh, to cry over.)

My father rented a horse and buggy and began to call on farmers around Woodstock. He took orders for pants and work clothes. When he had enough orders, he came to Toronto, to Spadina Avenue, and called cold on several manufacturers. One day the name Shiffer Hillman drew him into a factory. He met Mr. Shiffer and told him about the orders and asked for credit. He started to describe himself, and Mr. Shiffer stopped him in mid-sentence. "You don't need to explain anything," he said to my father. "Your face is your credit." Thank you, Mr. Shiffer. Years later, I had the pleasure of telling this lovely story to the Shiffer sons, Irv and Joe.

My father, Julius Shapiro, splendid in an elegant suit, courting my mother in New York, 1914

Julius Shapiro's relatives who brought him over to New York, c. 1910

In time, my father and mother opened Shapiro's Ladies' Wear at 488 Dundas Street, next door to the post office. In the early forties, Daddy was moved to do a singular thing. He arranged for a brass Star of David to be set into the granite at the entrance to the store. The premises have changed hands many times since, but the Star of David has survived to this day.

My mother made our dresses (with reinforced pockets to hold my collection of pebbles); we played in the street, crawled through concrete conduits under the railroad track. I had my first major sexual encounter in the garage of the house next door. By mutual agreement, six-year-old Charlie Bickle and I slipped into the garage, pulled the door closed. I said boldly, "I'll show you mine if you show me yours." After a moment's hesitation, Charlie lifted his shirt and I lifted mine. We each flashed the other a minuscule view of our belly buttons and then beat it out of the garage. There.

That part of my growing up Jewish in Woodstock now seems a dream of serenity, compared to what came later. We were the first Jewish family to settle in Woodstock. There was no community to join, and ours was the only house in the town not decorated for Christmas. I knew we were Jewish because my parents knew they were Jewish. But they had no way of knowing what we would experience in school, and it wasn't until I started this reminiscence and compared notes with my sisters that we learned we all three went through it but could not share the pain with one another. Don't ask me why. We each felt it was our own behaviour that was somehow to blame.

It began in Grade 1. What did the parents, the teachers, the churches teach at such an early age that six-year-olds could point to another six-year-old and yell with utter confidence that she had killed you-know-who? I was left-handed, and my kindergarten teacher, as she slapped my fingers, suggested it was a religious characteristic. We learned to dodge the bullies, but sometimes I would be ambushed riding my bike down a back lane to avoid confrontation. Grant McGinnis pushed me into the gravel behind our house at 596 Dundas Street. I still have the scar. Actually, I'm kind of proud of it and will show it to you if you want.

Getting to public school was an obstacle course, because I had to pass the dreaded steps of the YMCA. I would run up the back alley to the church. Once the Reverend Ashby saw me hesitating by the back door of the church, trying to get up the nerve to come round to the front. Mr. Ashby, understanding the situation, motioned me inside. He volunteered to act as lookout; he checked the steps, frowning across the road to the bullies. When the coast was clear, he led me out, guarded me, protected me. What a sweet memory.

It was harder again in high school. It was understood that no boy would ever walk with us, ride bikes with us, choose us for partners in games, and never, ever perform in any play that required them to kiss us. Ken Mooney said out loud to our drama teacher, "I don't have to kiss Beatrice, do I?" That little shit. He sat in front of me in Second Form, methodically scraping his scalp with his fingernails, then flicking the crop into the room. As the son of the minister of the Vansittart Avenue church, he was totally inaccessible to me, but I adored him.

High school was a disaster zone for us three Shapiro sisters. (My brother, Jackie, is six years younger. By the time he was eligible for high school, my parents had moved to Toronto, and he was spared the ignominy. Also, he was about six-feet-two-inches tall.) And yet, I was Humour Editor of the *Woodstock Oracle*; I won three dollars for my speech for the Oratorical Contest, "The Lost Continent of Something." I developed a life-long love of literature, fostered by my dear English teacher Miss Cropp. Similarly, I developed a life-long fear of math, fostered by math teacher Mr. Lawr, who called me Miss Scalisi. When I was carefully chosen to read the lines of a certain character in *The Merchant of Venice* (not by Miss Cropp!), desperate to avoid the titters, I smeared my throat with mercurochrome and showed it to the school nurse, who mercifully sent me home.

We were unable to inflict our distress on our parents, who could not know how it was to face the same adversaries day after day. We had a tragedy at home of such proportion that everything else paled by comparison. In the car one day, my little sister, Marion, was sitting cradled in Effie Taylor's arms. Effie helped my mother. Getting out of the car, she let Marion slip onto the brick sidewalk in front of City Hall. The baby didn't make a sound, and my mother screamed over and over, "Why doesn't she cry . . . ?" She never learnt to speak. She was irreparably brain-damaged. We all took turns protecting her, feeding her, changing her. We loved her passionately, but she was deteriorating, and my parents agonized over what to do, finally taking her to a hospital in Orillia. They operated and she died, a tiny, lovely wisp of life never lived.

I will not end on a sad note, and want to record my happiest memories of growing up Jewish in Woodstock. Or at least growing up. We often went to Port Stanley on a Sunday, and Mama packed marvellous picnics. The roast

Fanny Shapiro (right) in front of our store with Mrs. Lipowitz

Central Public School, Woodstock, early 1930s — Beatrice cosy in the front row (sixth from left)

chicken was always transported in the spotted blue enamel pan, tied up with a dishtowel. She baked apple and raisin pies, kugel, upside-down pudding. I remember my mother bending over the picnic, offering my father first choice, as always, and I am filled with tears. I remember something Adele Wiseman once said to me after Mama died. She had taken care of her mother for many years under her own roof. I had said to Adele that I didn't do my mother justice. She answered, "Don't worry. Your mother didn't do *her* mother justice." Well, it didn't exactly apply to my mother, but it comforted me anyway.

One of the rewards for bringing home good marks from school was a trip to Toronto, to Kensington Market. We travelled in a car called a Star, with mica windows. No heater. Daddy took burlap bags and he filled them with glorious treats: properly butchered chickens, sour pickles out of the barrels, schmalz herring, brains, sweetbreads, hearts, dried mushrooms on strings, miltz, great black bread from Lotmanns, and the live carp. I can't remember how we transported the carp, but I do remember it occupied the bathtub for a week. Mama was the one who had to despatch it. We all scattered. After a week a carp becomes a pet. Then it becomes gefilte fish.

My mother made her own noodles for her ineffable chicken soup; she baked the challah on Thursdays before she opened the store. Each day she prepared our meals, mediated our arguments. Jackie was a *mallach*; after four daughters came a son, and he could do no wrong. And actually he didn't. But we sisters, Goneril, Regan, and Cordelia . . . guess which I was. Francine washed the dishes, Ruth wiped, and I put away. Francine was the smartest, Ruth the most charming, and I the best looking. I always had to sit in the middle in the back-seat of the car, because I was the youngest. We fought a lot. Poor Mama. How did she ever open and close the store each day and still fill sparkling Mason jars with spiced peaches, bread-and-butter pickles, chili sauce, green tomatoes, cher-ries, jelly from grapes that grew over our summer kitchen? How did she find time to wrap all those apples and potatoes in newspaper and set them in saw-dust in the cold room? How did she do all that and still teach us songs we never heard anyone else sing? *Oh, once upon a time in Arkansas, an old man sat a-fiddling away* . . . that's fidd-l-ing. My father, who called my mother Wifey, said of her, she would be absolutely perfect if only she could sing like Alice Faye.

A born athlete! (1934)

The Hot Bath Couple, Freda and Falek Zolf, in the 1920s. They met and married in the stetl of Zastavia, in the Brest area of Russia, and Freda came alone to Canada on the S.S. Batory with her three children in 1926.

Hot Baths: The Fight of My Life

The classical Greek philosophers had taught me in college that man was a political animal. It was his politics that shaped his morality, his way of life. But these lessons in philosophy were neither new nor wondrous to me, for I knew that I alone in my college was a political entity long before my birth. Long before birth, I had a nose for politics, unrivalled in the Dominion of Canada, the City of Winnipeg, the universe.

Indeed, much of my actual birth consisted of my mother's long and sideways contractions intended to free my nose from its foetal containment. The outing of my nose was my mother's birth strategy.

Like the legendary dybbuk, my nose finally came out. It was my first outing, in the general maternity ward of St. Joseph's Polish Roman Catholic Hospital on Salter Street near Selkirk, very deep in the ghetto of ghettos, the North End of Winnipeg, the spiritual home of the Winnipeg General Strike and Canadian socialism.

It was a very difficult outing for both me and my mother. I came out of her womb nose first. The Polish nuns in attendance crossed themselves at the sight of my tiny little frame attached to such a huge honker. Even the portrait of Christ hanging above my mother's bed blinked in amazement.

Leibele (Larry) Zolf on his second birthday, not celebrated in the Zolf home on the grounds that birthdays were a gentile invention to lure the Jews to their doom, or so said Papa Zolf

For my mother, this nasal birth of her second son and her youngest was both an incredible and painfully endless journey. But finally, my mother gave birth to me, a unique, nine-pound-eight-ounce baby boy — unique in that my nose *alone* weighed nine pounds.

Having to steer a nine-pound nose through her uterus was trouble enough for my poor mother, but I did very little to help. My constant poking of my nine-pound nose into her every nook, cranny, and crevice on my way down and out of her womb was painful enough to put anyone off childbirth, even my mother.

Nevertheless, she was determined to give birth to my nine-pound nose. Of one thing she was certain: her Mezinik, her youngest son, possessed a mighty nose for greatness, handy perhaps for a useful place in the Rabbinate or as a nose-it-all champion of his people, or an eye, ear, nose specialist at the very least. With such a nose, she was sure her youngest could sniff out the truth in the most subtle of kabbalah secrets and sort out the trickiest Talmudic diatribes. With such a nose, her youngest could quickly expose the false and fair weather friends of Jewry and Jewry's enemies from within. My great baby proboscis could thus make me a nine-pound Nose Golem, a Jewish secret weapon and a bit of a redeemer, or so my mother fervidly believed.

Large, fleshy Jewish noses weighing nine pounds didn't really worry my mother. After all, I was not the first Jewish nine-pound nose in the family. In the Great War, my mother fell in love with a captain in Alexander Kerensky's Russian Revolutionary Army whose nose was so fleshy, so long, so powerful, so rubbery that he dug his own trench with it — and sometimes the trenches of the crazed and wounded around him.

When my father sneezed, he frightened many a German patriot into discarding his weapons and fleeing in terror. During military briefings, the large strategic maps of the Kerensky government were often hung from my father's nose. No one in Kerensky's Revolutionary Army could spot a poison gas attack faster than my father, Yoshua Falk Zolf Long Nose, First of the Hebrews.

My mother, the daughter of a well-off steel foundry owner, was a tall, dusky beauty, with a well-rounded figure and beautiful black eyes. Instinctively, my mother knew that a five-foot-six-inch Jewish Cyrano in hand as a suitor was better than two Paul Munis in the bush. She married Long Nose, whom she loved wildly, and dreamed of giving him a Long Nose child he could take

Papa Zolf, an officer in the Kerensky Army, spring 1917, relaxes with friends before he's sent to the German front (Pop is third from the right)

for walks or to picnics or could rub noses with, trying perhaps to set the world on fire in the process.

My mother's first three children all had button noses. My mother's disappointment in them was patent. She went into semi-mourning after each of her three perfect snub-nosed children was born. She longed for another Jewish Long Nose in the family.

Now at last, a second Long Nose was on the way. As she watched me and my nine-pound nose squirm out of her womb ever so slowly, she knew that at last a Nose for the Jews, a Nose for Canada, a Nose of Noses had arrived in the humble Zolf household on 180 Aikins Avenue. Long Nose, her husband, would be lonely no more.

I didn't know it at the time, but like many things in my life my birth was a political statement, my very first one and also my mother's. I was born on July 19, 1934, in the very heart of the Great Depression. My father, a school teacher in the Isaac Loeb Peretz School, a Yiddish socialist-Zionist school, already had three children to clothe, feed, and take to the movies. My sister Rose was thirteen, my brother Meyer was twelve, my sister Judy was eight.

An extra mouth to feed on his pittance of a salary was not what my father had been looking forward to. Both he and my mother were in their mid-forties. They were very much in love. My father felt it would be cheaper and more efficient for him to cuddle and caress my mother than to caress and cuddle a very hungry fourth child in the grimmest of Depression poverty.

At that time, my father was a socialist, a Zionist, and definitely a bit of a modernist. On the other hand, my mother was more than a titch Orthodox, always blessing Sabbath candles, always salting meat to get the blood out of it. My mother was also a faithful reader of the love romances in the New York Yiddish newspapers and a fervent believer in the Evil Eye, which she said was everywhere – even under the beds in Buckingham Palace.

But a modernist my mother certainly was not. She hated pressure cookers, automatic elevators, escalators, airplanes, and motor cars. The political correctness of the socialist was not for her, especially the socialist charge that Jewish Orthodoxy was the opiate of the Jewish people. Nor did she consider the free-love lifestyle of many of my father's socialist male and female bosses to be either edifying, proper, or correct. Nor did the mud and sands of Palestine the Zionists were busy draining hold any charms for her. My mother's Paradise, my mother's Golden Hesiodic Age, was at her father's huge, sprawling house by the lake in Poland, where she did the Australian crawl, the butterfly, the backstroke better than any woman in her village.

Looking homeward was almost a daily reflex for my mother. The fact that the fascist Pilsudski government of Poland and then the Nazis made her return impossible did not stop my mother from considering her village her one and only home sweet home.

Secretly, very secretly, my mother was also leery of feminism, especially socialist and Zionist feminism, which made Zionist and socialist women equal comrades with men in the class struggle for socialism and a Jewish Palestine. These Jewish feminists my mother found too brash, too tough, too dogmatic for her cautious, careful, perhaps paranoid world view. In particular, my mother hated the free-love Jewish socialist feminists who ran the dreaded Mother's Union of my father's school. It was these feminist terrors, my mother was told, who goaded and bullied the Jewish teachers who came before them.

Some Jewish teachers were peremptorily fired by the Mother's Union. Others had their sexuality questioned on a public platform or were publicly accused of slacking in their love of socialism, or of openly professing socialism and Zionism but secretly teaching their students Orthodoxy and other heresies.

The Mother's Union feminist powers of hiring and firing teachers or humiliating them or driving them batty turned my mother into a first-class fighter of feminism. At school gatherings, my mother would often excuse her-self and go to the cloakroom. There she stuck pins into Jewish-looking voodoo dolls, then called Jewdoo dolls, and put the Jewdoo dolls into the pockets of the coats belonging to the very wealthy members of the Mother's Union. In the sleeves of these coats, my mother put cloves of garlic, small vials of chicken fat, and a page from the Jewish Woman's Prayer Book in which Moses calls on the Israelites in the desert to stop sinning and behave themselves.

My father also dreaded the Wicked Witches of the Peretz School Mother's Union. But secretly he envied these women their sophistication, their ruthless pragmatism, their modernism. It was from these women that my father got the bright idea for coping with my mother's majestic announcement that she was pregnant and I was on my way.

My father insisted the Zolfs could not afford a fourth child. My father had a solution to the problem, a Jewish feminist solution. My father suggested to my mother that I, the foetus, be drowned before actual birth, in a rapid series of hot, very, very hot, baths.

In response to that hot bath diktat, my mother looked straight into the eyes of her husband, the abortionist. She went into the kitchen and stopped the clock; she spat in her hands twice; she spread chicken fat all over her face and threw a whole salt shaker over her left shoulder to ward off the works of the Evil One that had brought on my father's hot bath request. But my mother offered no active form of resistance to my father the abortionist – apart from passive resistance. Frankly, she loved Long Nose too much to do that.

Apparently, from then on, my mother took several hot baths a day. At least the family could hear the taps running upstairs and could see my mother carefully and demonstrably drying her hair downstairs shortly thereafter. Weeks and months passed. Soon my mother was constantly itching and scratching herself all over the place. Sometimes, too, there was an odd smell in a room that my mother had just left.

Even as a foetus, I had spotted that life-saving body odour of my mo-ther's. Even as a foetus, I loved my smelly mother madly. I just loved the juicy gossip tidbits and her secret plans for me that she whispered into my tiny, tiny foetus ears. I, the foetus, was told by my mother that she was so deter-mined to have me, she wasn't taking baths of any kind just to make sure my father the abortionist's grand design for me would be thwarted. Here I was, already the confidante of my gorgeous, voluptuous mother. Could any foetus

Little Mr. Leibele (Larry) Zolf, age 3

The wunderkind at 4

Senator-in-waiting, age 5

ask for anything more? Without fully understanding it then, my nose for the politics of abortion – my nose for politics – was already fighting for my life in my mother's womb.

When my mother talked to me about out-foxing my father, her husband the abortionist, I would give my mother a playful kick in her tummy or pass a little foetal wind to convey my approval for my mother's latest stratagems for deceiving my father and keeping me alive. I particularly liked my mother's little white lies, particularly the ones she told my father the abortionist. She said the reason she was gaining weight at a very rapid rate was because all her many, many hot baths made her perpetually hungry.

When I was finally delivered by Dr. Victor, the communist doctor, our neighbourhood Dr. Bethune, my mother's refusal to bathe for over nine months made me the smelliest baby ever born in Winnipeg, or Canada, or the world for that matter. With my nine-pound nose, I couldn't miss the pungent aroma of my very smelly mom, and I cried long and ferociously in outrageous response. Still, I was safe at last. My father the abortionist could now no longer drown me.

Naturally, this experience, a highly personal one in a very controversial area, made me leery of abortionists, their feminist socialist allies, and particularly my father the abortionist for many years to come. I howled like a banshee when my father tried to pick me up from my hospital crib and give me a cuddle. My sobbing never ended when my father took me in the baby carriage for a stroll on the treeless, gravel-sided streets of North Winnipeg. When my father leaned over into my baby carriage and tried to rub his schnoz against mine, my tiny hands shot up, grabbed his elephantine nose and refused to let go.

My mother quickly calmed the fears engendered by the first foray of my nose into politics, the very personal family politics of abortion. At this stage of my life, I was certainly a dyed-in-the-wool Right to Lifer. My mother, who had skilfully fought her abortion battle for the right of my nine-pound nose to live and breathe in the brisk fresh air of freezing Winnipeg, certainly understood my views on this matter and respected them even then. My mother kept me out of my father's clutches as much as she possibly could. When I, as a mere infant, responded in complete terror to the eerie, life-denying sounds of a hot tub being run for my father upstairs, it was my mother who was always there with sweets and a soother.

The university scholar, with mother, father, sister, and nephews

My mom was an understanding woman. When I reached maturity and became a celebrity TV journalist, at last my mother's views on women's rights and mine meshed completely. My love for my mother quickly translated into a love and respect for women in general (with the possible exception of the Mother's Union, of course). I quickly learned that if you're a man and truly love and respect women, you let women do with their own bodies what they wish. If you're a man and truly love and respect women, you also let women do with *your* body what they wish.

It was my love for my mother that also made me realize that my father was more than a mere would-be Jewish abortionist. Even as an infant, I realized how much my mom and dad loved each other. Besides, any man with a nine-pound nose very much like mine that was so loved by my very beautiful mother had to be a man who loved women as much as I did. Surprisingly, my love for my father the abortionist followed quicker than either of us had expected. Actually, I really couldn't help love that man of mom's. I was the spitting image of my father, and my own self-love dictated my love for him.

My father's nose was enormous and was dotted with carbuncles, warts, pimples, moles, and other fleshy apparitions. My father was really the first Nose That Walked Like a Man in North Winnipeg. And I managed to make my nose walk like a man too, from the glowing example my father had set before me in my childhood.

Besides, I had, quite by accident, come up with my own solution for my problem with Papa, a solution that let my father atone for his Original Sin against me, the sin of trying to prevent me from having a life. When I was about three or four, my father was asleep on the couch, snoring away loudly and rhythmically. Having nothing to do at the time, and being a very restless child, I decided to act out one of my favourite childhood fantasies, the one of the little Jewish socialist shoemaker tapping away at the shoes on his workbench.

I took a small hammer from the kitchen and a wooden matchstick. I placed the matchstick in my father's left ear, and, pretending it was a nail and my father's ear a shoe, I drove the matchstick very slowly right through his eardrum. I punctured the eardrum completely, nearly killing my father and finally costing him all hearing in his left ear.

When my father came out of the ether at the hospital, he did something I didn't expect. He forgave me completely. Perhaps he did so because he was soon to discover that he could hear better out of one ear than anyone else out of two.

Perhaps he forgave me because I could at age three or four already speak English and Yiddish fluently, read and write Hebrew completely, and play child parts in Yiddish plays that came on tour to Winnipeg from New York.

Perhaps my father also forgave me because in those Depression days, Canada was so pernicious a society and so politically incorrect. In those days it was simply assumed that a three- or four-year-old child who drove a matchstick through his father's eardrum was too young to know what he was doing and certainly too young to feel any guilt. It was this assumption that led my parents to keep this episode a secret from me until my Bar Mitzvah at age thirteen, when I was considered man enough to know about my Darkest Hour.

I was lucky. It was the Dirty Thirties and I was deemed to be a naive innocent. I was lucky because my father forgave me. My father was lucky too. Now, in my books, my father had at last atoned for his hot-water abortionist sins against me. In my inner heart, I forgave my father totally and completely. I of course could not tell him that at the time, because my father would have to wonder how a three- or four-year-old knew so much about hot-bath abortions of foetuses in the first place.

Instead, since the matchstick-in-the-eardrum episode, my father and I became the closest of pals. Day in and day out, he couldn't help showing how glad he was that I was still alive, even though I was a fourth mouth to feed. Sometimes I wondered about all that when I saw his baleful look as I consumed huge globs of borscht, blintzes, verenekes, kreplach, and kasha by the bowl, every day, day in and day out, as if it was all good Jewish Gerber's baby soul food.

In my childhood, I was the apple of my father's eye, the sound of music in my father's one functioning ear. I went everywhere he went. I stood beside him as we devoured pastrami sandwiches, played chess, went to the Yiddish theatre, made Yiddish speeches in Peanut and Stella parks. I was my father's Boswell. I was my father's pet little prodigy, who would soon deliver the Jews of North Winnipeg at last from their poverty, their sorrows, their pinched and narrow lives.

To help me in that sacred task, my father had given me his fleshy, bulbous nose — a nose I joyously rubbed in politics, particularly Jewish politics.

Friends on Beatrice Street, 1938 (Back row, left to right: Sammy Lasky, Harold Amster, Alan Feldman, Maxie Applebaum, Fred Sharf, Johnny Murphy, unidentified. Front row, left to right: Davie Silverman, Al Reisman, Freddy Reisman)

FRED SHARF

Beatrice Street and the Pits Gang

A recent television documentary titled "The Riot at Christie Pits" took me back to my youth on Beatrice Street and reawakened memories of the Pits Gang, a group of anti-Semitic bullies that terrorized the area. The 1933 Christie Pits riot is an event well known to my contemporaries in Toronto's Jewish community. But after fading into the past for decades, it has now re-emerged as a topic of historical interest for our children — and the larger community. And yet, the TV film made it seem as though this riot was a one-time incident. In fact, it was one incident in an ongoing war. Christie Pits was a war zone throughout the 1930s and for the first two years of the Second World War. During that time local police did nothing whatsoever to protect citizens in this part of Toronto. Too much has still been left unsaid. However unbelievable the stories may now seem to my sons and their friends in a 1990s Toronto, I want them to hear about the Pits Gang, and about how it was for me and my friends. This, then, is my tale.

I grew up on Beatrice Street, part of an old working-class neighbourhood in the College, Grace, Crawford area of Toronto. I lived there from the early thirties until the war years. The boys I grew up with on Beatrice Street were the

My friends on Beatrice Street, from Maxie's album, 1936 (Back row, left to right: Sammy Lasky, Maxie Applebaum, Alan Feldman, Hank Robertson. Front row, left to right: Fred Sharf, Bobby Robertson, Johnny Murphy)

best friends anyone could have. We are still friends, and, although our lives have led us in many different directions, we still get together regularly. The boys on Beatrice Street hung out together. That meant playing together and protecting each other. We had a leader named Maxie Applebaum. Today, Maxie is still the leader; he is the one to organize the yearly reunions, spending hours on the telephone to make sure everyone shows up.

Toronto in those days was a city of approximately 500,000 people, collected in residential pockets. It was truly a city of neighbourhoods. There could be three or four streets inhabited mostly by Italian people (Clinton Street, Claremont Street, etc.), and then three or four streets with a large Jewish population (Beatrice Street, Grace Street, etc.). Heading east from Beatrice, there must have been a dozen of these mini-neighbourhoods, whose parks bustled with activity — since television was not yet invented. There was no crime as we know it. The streets were safe. Kids formed neighbourhood gangs, but the word "gang" did not hold the dangerous connotation it does today. The "Jersey" gang and the "Bellwoods" gang, to name two, were made up of tough guys and bullies, but they were not anti-Semitic. If one guy in our gang knew one guy in the Bellwoods gang then we could safely walk through "their" territory to the Kiwanis Club, or to Mr. Forman's or Mr. Kopel's Cheder (Hebrew and religion class), both of which were located in Bellwoods park.

Then there was the Pits Gang. They were truly anti-Semitic, seeking out Jews and attacking whenever their members outnumbered ours by three or four to one. Like Apaches in a Hollywood movie, they would swoop down from the top of the ravine and brutally beat up anyone who made the mistake of lingering in their path.

The riot that was featured recently on television broke out at a baseball game in Christie Pits in 1933. It occurred during a game between a non-Jewish team and a Harbord playground team that was mostly Jewish. The riot started in the stands when some hostile fans unfurled a swastika banner, and the ensuing battle turned into probably the bloodiest ever fought in this neighbourhood "war zone."

At the time, I was an eight-year-old boy living at 203 Beatrice Street, halfway between College Street and Beatrice Park. I still have etched in my memory, as if it were yesterday, a picture of the battered and bloody "walking wounded" who made their way south on Beatrice Street, away from the war zone into the safety of our neighbourhood.

In 1940 (left to right: Hank Robertson, Alan Feldman, Maxie Applebaum)

But the fighting – and the fear – did not end that 1933 day at Christie Pits. Throughout the 1930s, the area's three parks were wide open spaces, free of the buildings they hold today. Jews were considered safe in the southernmost, Beatrice Park, which ran from the top of Beatrice Street north to Harbord Street. It had a number of tennis courts, which in the winter were converted into a huge outdoor skating rink. Many Jewish boys and girls enjoyed these facilities. For our gang, this park became headquarters. It was almost a second home. And yet everyone who enjoyed Beatrice Park knew better than to linger when the crowds thinned out, because occasionally the Pits Gang would cross Harbord Street to see if they could catch a few stragglers and beat them up.

The next park up, running north from Harbord Street almost to Bloor Street, was known as Bickford Park. It was the most dangerous, because it was built in a deep ravine – a perfect trap for the predatory Pits Gang. Bickford Park was the site of some savage battles up to the years of the Second World War. Adjoining Bickford Park to the north was Christie Pits. That was Pits Gang territory, and Jewish people dared not enter it under usual circumstances. The only exception might be, for instance, when a Jewish ball team played in the park with a large number of Jewish spectators on hand – which was the case on that day of the notorious 1933 riots.

I played on the YMHA team in a baseball league from 1938 to 1940, and all of our home games were held in Bickford Park. We had a very strict rule, which we obeyed to the letter: when the game was over, the team members had to leave together, as a group – with no stragglers. There was safety in numbers, and

In 1940 (Back row, left to right: Harry Feldman, Phil Elias, Sollie Goldmon. Front row, left to right: Irving Applebaum, Fred Sharf, Oscar Markovitz)

everyone made sure this rule was never broken. That is why I have no memory of ever being attacked when we left that park after one of our ball games.

That all changed about two years later, probably in 1942. One beautiful summer evening, Georgie Riesman, Maxie Applebaum, and I had just finished watching a baseball game in Bickford Park. As usual after a game, the park emptied quickly, and we were left sitting on the grass at the top of the hill for a matter of minutes. We should not have lingered there at all, but I guess we got involved in our talk and made a mistake — a very costly mistake, as we were about to find out. At first I gave it little thought, because I was with Maxie, and with Maxie I always felt secure. He was tough and never backed away from a confrontation.

Suddenly, a boy of about thirteen or fourteen years old came down and asked us for the time. At that moment we knew we were in deep trouble. This had happened to us before. The boy was a scout for the Pits Gang, and we knew at once what lay before us. Just then, from several different directions, members of the gang appeared. We were sixteen or seventeen years old, out-numbered by at least five to one, and among the attackers was a big, older brute wearing a Canadian army uniform.

We started moving up the hill, but by the time we reached the top, Maxie and the soldier were fighting. I was surrounded by five or six gang members and was fighting for my life against a guy wearing a "taxi" hat. During the struggle, other members of the gang, who were surrounding me, closed in and pushed me down. They kicked me in the face. My lower lip and the inside of my mouth were bleeding and I knew I was in great danger. I looked around and saw Maxie fighting three or four gang members, led by the big soldier. Georgie, trapped in a predicament much like mine, was getting badly beaten. He motioned to Maxie and me to take off. Georgie and I managed to get loose and make a mad dash across Harbord Street. Once we were into Beatrice Park, our pursuers gave up the chase. But Maxie was not with us! He did not, or could not, get away. We had to get help in a hurry.

Georgie and I ran down Beatrice Street, shouting to every person we met about what was going on with Maxie and the Pits Gang in Bickford Park. Georgie ran to his father's fruit and grocery store at the corner of College Street, where he rounded up his dad, his brother, and a few others who happened to be on College Street at the time. It did not take very long to summon a large group and head back into the park to rescue Maxie. The Pits Gang dispersed as soon as they saw us. Maxie was lying on the ground, punched, pummelled, and beaten. He was almost unrecognizable, but being Maxie, he was still hanging on to the soldier. We grabbed the soldier and led him south to Beatrice Street. Someone called the police. Slowly, Pits Gang members began to appear, two or three at a time, filtering out of the back lanes.

But then the police arrived and took charge — so to speak. They looked at Maxie, beaten like nobody I had ever seen, or have ever seen since. They looked at Georgie and myself, both thoroughly battered and bleeding. What did "Toronto's finest" do? Did they put anyone in jail? Did they report the Canadian soldier to his army unit? No. This was 1942 and this was a Jewish/Italian street. Let me tell you what the police did do. One officer noticed that an onlooker had an expired licence on his bicycle, so the policeman gave him a ticket. That was all. No arrests of Pits Gang members — not even a warning. That was about all you could expect back then.

Three years later, in 1945, I was in the Canadian Armed Forces, stationed in Doorn, Holland. The war had been over for about eight weeks, and I was on night duty, guarding an army dump filled with captured trucks, guns, and other spoils of war. Standing next to me, at the entrance to this dump, was a soldier from another company also assigned to guard duty. We had a long night ahead of us, and so we began to talk. I spent the whole night talking to Rifleman Archer. I was surprised to find out that not only was he from

The world is at war, and the boys are old enough to enter the armed services. Beatrice Street is represented in all the services, army, navy, and air force. (left to right: Oscar Markovitz, Sollie Goldmon, RCAF, Fred Sharf, Sollie Raibman, RCAF)

Bunny Silverman, RCN

Alan Feldman, RCAF

Lawrence Granovsky, RCA

Fred Sharf, RCA

The war ends and the good life begins

Toronto, he was from my own part of town. And not only was he from the very same district, he was a member of the Pits Gang! I was shocked at this strange coincidence. Here I was, standing just eight feet away from a member of the Pits Gang. He was my former enemy and yet we wore the same uniform in the same regiment.

"Archer, I can't imagine you as a member of the Pits Gang," I remember saying. "Why would you choose to join a gang devoted to beating up Jews?"

He told me that when he was a young teenager, he took an oath to keep Jews out of Christie Pits and Bickford Park. Why did he take such an oath? I asked him. Had he ever met any Jews who had caused him harm? He answered that I was the first Jew he had ever spoken to. As for why he took the oath, he merely repeated all the anti-Semitic stereotypes he had heard about Jewish people. By the end of the night, after eight hours of talking on many different subjects, in spite of ourselves we felt a bond. I truly think that Archer realized that night that his ignorant beliefs had been fundamentally challenged. He had become friendly with the only Jew he had ever met. And for eight hours I had a friendly discussion with a member of the Pits Gang — a group that had terrorized me for years. A month later, Rifleman Archer was found drowned in a canal in Holland. I felt genuinely sorry when I heard the news.

Michael Wex at Massey College, Toronto

Oy Canada

I f only my father had had the courage to throw back his leonine, Talmudic head in what the goyim, the *ethical* goyim, would call a frenzy of legalistic rage, point his forefinger out the door, and say unto me with the ossified implacability of all the ages, "*Avek fin mayn tir*, depart this house, you jazz singer, you," while my mother sat weeping in the corner, smashing every Yossele Rosenblatt '78 in his cantorial record collection;

If only a shelfful of Talmud had caved in upon me one day, leaving my *goyisher kop* forever addled;

If only Tradition had barfed me forth onto the dry sands of Western Civilization, I could have grown up into a big shot, a contender: a stammering, nattering, chest-pulling Jewish intellectual with nothing on my mind but social justice and yellow-haired *shiksas*, the hero of a thousand novels.

But on account of my sins I was pulled out of the dress rehearsal for the Major C. E. Douglas Collegiate Institute Christmas and New Year's Gala — participation compulsory if you wanted to pass music — just as I was stepping into the spotlight. Blacked-up like a pair of Passover shoes, a derby hat clutched to the heart of my red vest, my *payess*, my sidelocks, tucked up inside a curly wig, I was in the middle of the chorus, the *solo chorus*, of "I Want a Girl

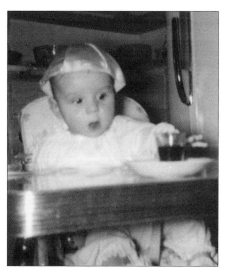

Waiting for Shabbes, March 1955

Mixed bathing — first step to perdition, July 1955

Just Like the Girl," when into the gym comes my father, hopping and twitching and flapping his arms, ignoring the screams of the teacher to run right up and drag me from the gym in full sight of twenty-five other giggling minstrels. "A family emergency," he yelled to the teacher. And to me, *"Zulst zakh sheymen in vaytn haldz, khomer-ayzl,* music-lover, bum!"

My poor father — with all his other problems, he had to have me, too. A man of his education, stuck inside a candy store in Coalbanks, Alberta, and he wanted to be somebody, yet. Nu, go be somebody in the middle of nowhere, *in goles afileh fin goles,* in exile even from the Exile. What could he do? He could run the only *shoymer shabbes,* the only Sabbath-observant candy store between Winnipeg and the Rockies; he could run the only candy store in the world to smell of gallnuts, the stuff they use to make the ink for Torahs, tefillin, and mezuzahs; he could become the town's scribe and cantor and still have time to run his candy store twelve hours a day.

The gallnuts were bad enough, but with his passion for righteousness, it could go you dark in the eyes. For him it was already too late; but me, I was gonna be a great rabbi, just like the rest of his family. I was a Jew with beard and sidelocks, thank God. Well, a Jew, anyway. With sidelocks. And hidden away in the midst of my father's cantorial records — Rosenblatt, Sirota, Leibele Waldman, he had them all — hidden away there, one, just one, unprepossessing little bombshell: Elvis Presley. And in my bedroom, between the mattress and the box spring, where my mother wouldn't find it — go know she'd lift up the mattress when she went to make the bed — one copy, slick and nearly new, one copy — *Gotenyu,* my hands still tremble just thinking about it — of *Nudist Life.* Shmiley Greenberg gave it to me after I found him abusing his *tsitsis* one day. Elvis, nudists — I may have had *payess,* but I was hip. Who the hell wanted to be a rabbi and spend his life deciding which chickens were kosher and which had to be thrown away? I knew what *I* wanted. I was going to be the nudist Elvis Presley, performing only in nudist camps, singing "Heartbreak Hotel" to audiences full of girls, women, female babies, who didn't care if I gazed upon their nakedness — my God, they *wanted* I should look — and who I didn't care if they saw what I had. A rabbi? I'd seen *our* laundry: *shelkes* and petticoats and *inthoyzn* and *maytkes* and *halkes* and bloomers — are there even English words for these things? — a regular Eaton's catalogue of horrors from 1903, and we even had indoor plumbing, yet. A rabbi? Peh. Unless, unless I could start a new kind of Hasidism, me, Yoine Vekslbaum, the *davening* Jewish nudist with his ballbearing hips, and *daven* and sing Yiddish folksongs to roomsful of girls, women . . .

Nudist? I didn't even get my coat on. My father shlepped me outta there in a headlock, my head and shoulders buttoned up inside his coat and my *tukhes* exposed to the prairie wind. My Hebrew name might be Jonah, but if *Pinocchio* was any indication, I'd rather have been swallowed by a whale than locked up inside my father's winter coat. The stink of mothballs and sweat in there, the taste of his shirt between my teeth, the bounce bounce bounce of my head against his chest — I was carsick already. He smoked cigars from his own store, three for a dime, and he stank like a club car. I couldn't tell anymore if my tears were from terror or the stench. My lips and teeth were covered with the residue of my make-up, and by the time we got home the rest of Al Jolson was on my father's white shirt.

"Sit down, *Reb Noyef*, Mr. Lecher," and he threw me into a chair. My mother came in from the kitchen, her face the colour of cheesecloth. "Nu, Rokhel, *kim shoyn. Reb Noyef* has to leave soon. *Reb Noyef hot* an appointment in a nudist colony."

My mother spoke up. "Shaye, take it easy. He's only a boy."

"Boy? A pig lies in the mud waving its cloven hooves in the air and cries, 'Eat me, I'm kosher.'. . . Boy? This isn't a boy, it's a Presley with *payess*."

I wanted the earth to swallow me up like it had done to Korah the son of Yitzhar.

"While his parents are breaking their backs he shouldn't have to spend his life in a candy store doling out poison to vipers, what has this, this *boy* been sneaking into the house? Spinoza? Comic books? Hmmph — for heresy, for idiocy, this one is too good. Not Spinoza, not comic books, not Karl Marx or Bergson. So what then, what has he been sneaking in, his parents aren't looking?" And he held up my copy of "Heartbreak Hotel." "Elvis Shaygets Presley, the lascivious howler, the bom that not even a goy like Ed Solomon wants should be on his parade of television foolishness. And where do you think he's been sneaking it? You would think that even Mr. Insolent Stiff Neck would have the decency to hide such garbage under his dirty laundry or with his library of fine art books." I winced. "But no, not this one. Right here, right here between Yossele Rosenblatt singing 'Eli Eli' and Jan Peerce's 'A Din Toyre Mit Got,' here resides the son of Belial singing, what is it? 'Heartbreak Hotel.'

"Now, my son," and he turned to me gently. "Let me *fartaytsh* you, let me explain for you the meaning of this saying of your sage Rabbi Elvis ben Orleh, Elvis the son of foreskin, 'heartbreak hotel.' Heartbreak, in Jewish this is *a tse-brokhen harts*. And a hotel? *An akhsanye*, a place where you stay for only a night.

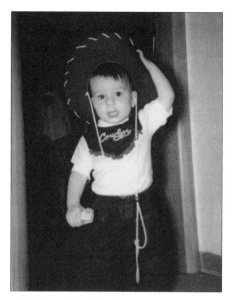

Fulfilling the local traditions, January 1957

The Lethbridge I remember

Now, what is another way of saying that somebody is with a *tsebrokhen harts?* Correct, that the event itself is *hartsraysendik.* And what means *hartsraysendik?* Something *vus rayst oop ba emetsn dus harts,* which rips somebody's heart out. And where does this tearing out of the heart take place? *Takeh* in the *akhsanye,* the place where you stay for only a night. Nu, *my ka mashmo lan?* What does this teach us? A deep and profound moral lesson: that before I throw you out of this house for once and for all, I'm going first to rip your heart from your chest for killing your mother and me, *farshteyst?* Heart, veins, arteries, the whole story straight from your chest, and leave it for the dogs, like the blood of the wicked in the days of the prophets. Any questions thus far?"

I shook my head mutely and wished I were dead. "Good. Mr. Wolf-in-Sheep's-Clothing understands everything. But don't leave yet, Whose-Mind-Is-Lower-Than-Mud. In a minute from now you'll tell me all about women. But first we'll bring this business to a close." And he held up my copy of "Heartbreak Hotel," and he read off the title again, and he read off the writing credit and the time and the label and the serial number, and he dropped one hand and with the other flung the record at me with all his strength. "Heartbreak Hotel," the unread Torah of my youth; "Heartbreak Hotel," which I'd never even had a chance to play, defiled by the hands of an unbeliever. Arise, O Lord, and let thine enemies be scattered.

But all that scattered were the pieces of my record. After it bounced off my nose and my father had finished beating me over the head with it, he threw it to the floor and stomped it to a thousand pieces. My mother was screaming, my father was yelling, I was crawling around the floor, trying to salvage the relics of my normalcy. My mother was telling my father that he should shut up, that the Angel of Silence should take him and all his sainted forebears to all the black years. "You'll sacrifice your son to Elvis Presley? *Bist dan a tuter un nish'ka futer,* you're a Tatar, not a father. A father punishes, a father doesn't kill." My father answered her something in Polish. I tried to crawl out of the room, but my mother grabbed me by the collar and held me to. They went back to Yiddish. "This magazine, Shaye, it's six months old already. Tell me, in six months has the boy grown a foreskin?"

"Not for want of trying," said my father.

I gazed hopefully down my chest. "Stand up," said my mother. "And stop looking at the floor."

I was supposed to explain myself now. I knew what I was supposed to say, but how was I supposed to stand there with half my head in blackface and tell them I wanted to be like everybody else? I couldn't stand everybody else, not there in Coalbanks, not in Williamsburg, Brooklyn, where they used to call me cowboy and *shaygets* – "Hey cowboy, *vus makhn di ferd*, how are your horses?" – not anybody or anything in the whole wide world which God had created according to His will. My parents wanted to hear about my boyish curiosity, and all I could think about was how much I hated everybody and everything around me. Jews, goyim, mailboxes, lampposts, the novels and comics and *gemoreh* and occasional movies that served me as friends – the whole thing burst over me like a sudden storm. "I wanna be a success with women," I wailed. "I wanna win friends and influence people."

"And we're stopping you?" asked my father. "We want you should have friends. But how's this *shmuts* gonna help?"

I didn't know. I didn't even know why I'd said it, except that I had to say something. "Well . . . well, *nem-zhe lemushel*, the girls, like take the girls, for instance. How'm I ever gonna find out about this stuff? I mean, they even talk about it in the Torah, and I still don't know what it's all about."

My parents both winced. The older I got, the more prone I was becoming to talk English in Yiddish words. "Yoinele, *konst nisht reydn a laytish mameh-lushn?*"

"All right, all right. But if I don't find out about this stuff somewhere – *ir vilt yakh zul oysvaksn in a pimp*, I should grow up to be a pimp?"

My parents were staring at me as if they'd gone into the Louvre and found Milton Berle where the Mona Lisa should be. "*Bist metiref gevoren in gantsn*, you gone completely crazy? What's this with the pumps all of a sudden?"

In the heat of my eloquence, in the middle of my King's Yiddish, I called a pimp a pimp, forgetting that to my parents a pimp was a thing that water came out of on farms. "It's English. A pimp . . . " we didn't talk about that sort of thing at home, so I explained to my parents what I thought a pimp was. They got the general idea and then they explained to me, since I was such a man of the world, exactly why pimps became pimps.

My disappointment was all the answer they needed. "Nu, *pimpele*," said my mother, "Nu, my little pump, forget all this foolishness and go back to school. I'll give you a note."

They'd forgotten how my father had dragged me home, and I could see this was no time to remind them. So I ran like hell the six blocks back to Major Douglas, my hand holding onto my yarmulke, my *payess* flapping in the wind.

*My father, Allan, and
me (at about age 17),
Sault Ste Marie, c. 1944*

Room and Keyboard

The boy in the *New Yorker* advertisement is about nine or ten. Well-scrubbed and neatly attired, he's the kind of kid you see on a Saturday at F.A.O. Schwarz's being presented with an expensive birthday toy by an adoring grandmother from Scarsdale. He stands with one hand boyishly tucked in his trousers pocket, the other resting casually on a piano bench, all poise and self-assurance, a typical young Manhattanite who divides his time between penthouse and private academy. The copy beneath the picture glows with high hope: "He'll be playing a Steinway, the piano played by most professional pianists, which should add some incentive to his practice hours." The writer of this bit of prose may know a great deal about pianos and piano virtuosi. What he knows about boys, on the other hand, doesn't amount to a hemidemisemiquaver.

I stare at the advertisement and suddenly I am the boy in the picture. It is October, 1935. Voices are speaking to me, at me, over me, and around me.

"What do you mean you don't want to learn to play the piano?"

"Everybody nowadays plays piano —"

"Show me one house in this town that doesn't have a piano?"

The voices, rising in pitch and intensity with each delivery, are those of my mother and father. It is Saturday, lunchtime. The table bears leftovers from

My parents, Allan and Janey Torgov, in their engagement photo, Winnipeg, 1926

last night's traditional Friday night supper, reheated except for the remainder of a chicken which we eat cold with H.P. Sauce. A traditional Saturday lunch. It will soon be time for my parents to return downstairs to the store to make the final push for the week. ("If you don't make a dollar on Saturdays, you might as well close up altogether.") More important to me, the Saturday matinee at the Algoma Theatre begins in less than an hour. Burgess, my redheaded freckled friend will soon be knocking at the door. There will be a dime for the movie, a nickel for a chocolate bar, and a couple of hours of re-enacting with Burgess that day's episode of the Tarzan serial after the show is over and we are let out blinking in the late afternoon sun. Why can't they just let me eat my cold chicken and H.P. Sauce and leave me in peace?

This is the fourth or fifth meal in a row during which I've been forced to sit through these persuasions. I look anxiously at the kitchen clock. One thirty. A half-hour to go before the lights go out in the Algoma and that marvellously menacing M.G.M. lion flashes onto the screen, its impatient roar drowned out by cheering and whistling and stamping feet. The voices continue, pressing, reasoning, unreasoning.

"Remember *Top Hat*? The minute you came out of the movie you knew every song by heart, some even with the words! Fred Astaire didn't even sing them so good. I'm telling you you got a brilliant ear. It's a shame not to use it."

"And it'll be fun. Your father'll play his violin and you'll play the piano and the two of you can perform at parties sometimes."

Compared to glorious freedom in the streets of Sault Ste. Marie, the idea of musical togetherness at home is hardly a temptation. Even less tempting is the prospect of a father-and-son act. I see my father looking benignly down at me over the bow of his instrument, and I see myself in a velvet suit (like Freddy Bartholomew but even less appealing because I wear eyeglasses) playing dainty little trills and being hugged by bosomy old women and cheek-pinched by their paunchy old husbands. I'm the darling of the Sunday afternoon tea-and-spongecake set. What will my boyfriends say? It is almost too horrible to think of. Indeed, so overcome am I by the horror of it that tears form, collect around the lower rims of my glasses, and roll down my cheeks, dropping one by one into my soup. My mother prudently slides the soupbowl out of range. "It's salty enough already," she says.

Now they are reminding me that Irving Cohen, who lives a couple of blocks away, is only a year or two older than I and already he is in Grade Eight of the Toronto Conservatory piano course. The comparison infuriates me. Why must I always be compared to kids who are totally abnormal, kids who will engage willingly in the most unnatural activities just to ingratiate themselves with their elders? Irving Cohen, whom I have by turns scorned or ignored in our chance meetings, is now Private Enemy Number One on my list. Angrily I cry out, "I don't care what Irving Cohen does! I hate Irving Cohen!"

Finally comes that last-resort word — please. "Please," my father urges, "just take one lesson and see how you like it."

"But we haven't even got a piano," I argue back, hopelessly, my voice choking into a pitiful squeak.

"We'll get one. I'll look in the paper. Somebody always has a piano for sale."

Burgess stands in the doorway slapping his tweed cap against his thigh. It is late and he is impatient. I rush past him, my glasses tear-stained, and he turns, bewildered, to run after me. In my hand I clutch a dime for the movie, a nickel for the chocolate bar, and an extra dime — ten whole cents! — to spend as I please.

I have given up, caved in, knuckled under. I will be a piano player.

It is one week later. I have come home from school to find a piano standing in the hallway outside our apartment, like some strange timid monster waiting to be invited inside to become part of the family. Once the struggle to squeeze the piano through the front door is over, my parents stand back, appraising their latest acquisition.

"I think we got a bargain at thirty-five dollars," my father says.

"Yes, but don't forget you had to pay the movers on top of that," my mother says, a strong hint of disapproval in her tone.

My father defends himself. "I couldn't help it. The old lady said she needed thirty-five dollars clear to bail her son out of jail." But my mother is unconvinced. "I still think you could've made a deal for twenty-five. We're not millionaires, you know."

Not millionaires indeed. Still, in these arid penny-pinching times, when it is often difficult to find a chicken in every Jewish pot, how customary it has become to find a piano in every Jewish living room! Our home will follow this pound-foolish custom, except that the huge ugly-brown instrument — after being denied lodging in the living room (too cramped), in my parents' bedroom (too private), in the kitchen (too cluttered) – finally ends up in my bedroom at the rear of the apartment.

That room – windowless, sharing a frosted-glass skylight with the adjoining kitchen – exists in a state of half-darkness even on the brightest days. It is an area that begs for more sun and a bit of breeze. Instead it now receives within its four walls this gloomy monolith, keys yellowed and chipped, innards thickly coated with dust, and a middle A that probably hasn't vibrated four hundred and forty times per second since the day it was first struck at the factory.

"Where did the old lady keep it?" my mother asks, screwing up her nose. "The whole piano smells like bacon grease."

"I'll fix that soon enough," my father assures her, and promptly dumps a bag of mothballs through the top of the piano. I can hear them cascading through the strings and springs and hammers.

My mother screws up her nose again. "Now it smells like bacon grease and mothballs," she says.

What can this hideous piece of furniture possibly add to my life that I should be forced to cohabit with it? I think about the old lady's son and how lucky he'd been in jail. Imagine, a cell without a piano.

My father hisses obscenities in six Eastern European languages as he scrapes and rubs and polishes the instrument. The piano-tuner (who swears in English only) seizes one tool, hurls down another, mutters angry orders to himself, pounds middle A with his right index finger until both finger and note are exhausted. Finally, the strings have been tamed and the tuner puts down his pliers, seats himself at the keyboard, clears his throat, and plays at full volume one chorus of "I Love Coffee, I Love Tea." My mother laughs with amusement, and my father urges the tuner to play another chorus. I stay well in the background, praying that this toolbag Paderewski will fracture his fingers.

Now there is a man seated next to me on the piano bench. His hands, bony and bluish (he has walked over a mile in the raw November night to give me my first lesson), rest on the keys and he explains in a cultured English accent that I must pretend I am holding an orange in each of my hands. I can smell Sen-Sen on his breath as he examines my outstretched fingers the way a gourmet examines fresh beef to see if it's properly marbled. "We'll have to get rid of that webbing between your fingers," he says, looking solemn, like a surgeon about to cut. "At the moment your hands look like duck's feet."

My parents in their first car
(a Model T Ford), 1927

"The Cohens told us that their Irving had the same trouble with his hands at first," my father says.

"Lots and lots of good solid practice, that's what does the trick," the teacher says. Father and teacher nod solemnly. The rapport between them, established only minutes ago, is now centuries old.

"Irving Cohen does a half-hour in the morning before school, fifteen minutes at lunch, and a whole hour at night. And on Saturdays and Sundays he sometimes plays two hours straight without a stop." As he recites these statistics my father looks grimly at me, I look grimly at the teacher who in turn looks grimly at my father. We are, the three of us, a new phenomenon in the world of music – The Grim Trio. I am miserable, but presently misery gives way to hatred. I hate Irving Cohen even more now. And I realize that he and I are now destined to become rivals. My father is already burnishing the family armour. "Don't worry," he tells the piano teacher, "just give this kid of mine a year and he'll be up to Irving Cohen. The whole town'll be talking about him."

It is two years later. We are in the Foresters Hall, a large, draughty room which ordinarily serves the Jewish community as a place of worship, but which tonight has been transformed into a theatre with a low, hastily constructed stage, a curtain consisting of several white bedsheets, and some blue and white paper streamers draped in a limp and unimaginative fashion from the light fixtures on the ceiling. The final curtain has been drawn on the annual Purim play, the last curtain calls have been taken by the child stars, and the proud parents in the audience are busily trading compliments. There follows a short, musical concert. One untalented child after another steps sheepishly to centre-stage. Some sing songs, two young violinists scrape together a duet, the melody of which begins uncertainly and disappears entirely by the third or fourth bar. A trumpet player threatens to blast down the walls of Jericho for a second time in history. Everyone is off-key.

Now the master-of-ceremonies stands at centre-stage, beaming back at the roomful of beaming parents. "The time has come to hear from Ahasuerus and Haman," he announces. This introduction greatly amuses the audience, and the master-of-ceremonies is very pleased with his little joke. I, too, feel satisfaction, for in my role as King Ahasuerus I have had the pleasure on this night of condemning the evil villain, Haman – played by Irving Cohen – to hang. The sight of Irving being dragged off to the gallows has provided me with spiritual uplift, and I recall praying that he would stumble from the stage and crash-land right on his web-free fingers.

Haman, having suffered a humiliating death in the play, is invited to play the piano first, a courtesy which I welcome in the belief that he who plays last, plays best. Irving is seated at the piano. He is too shy to turn and face his audience, and merely mumbles over his shoulder the title of the piece he will play. No one quite catches the title, and I manage only to catch the words "by Johann Sebastian Bach." (I learn later by peeking at his music book that it is a prelude and fugue.) His fingers are swift and accurate. And the voices in the fugue mesh with the precision of well-tooled gears, the whole piece building strongly to a stirring, concluding major chord. There is a moment of silence. Rising from the piano bench, Irving turns and bows stiffly. The audience is cold; this has been cerebral music, music that is not of the heart. The applause, therefore, is merely polite and dies quickly. Irving moves awkwardly across the stage before the silent crowd and returns to his seat.

"His teacher's that German fellow," someone whispers.

"Goddam Germans. They're all alike. Everything comes out like from a machine," another responds.

"And now King Ahasuerus, please," the master-of-ceremonies calls, milking the situation for one more laugh.

I begin to play the opening phrases of Johann Strauss' "Tales of the Vienna Woods," and as I pass into the main theme, an "ah!" of recognition rises from the crowd. I have chosen wisely and I play the piece reasonably well, schmaltzing up my performance by playing the waltz rhythm of the left hand "rubato" in the shameless style of a band of gypsy restaurant musicians. Rustling leaves and chirping birds flow from my right hand. We are so deeply immersed in the Viennese woods that one or two people in the room are moved to hum or whistle along with me. I cannot spot my father and mother among the patrons, but vanity tells me they must be exploding with pleasure. The last grand chords bring down the house.

But I do not stop to accept the accolade; instead I rush off the stage and out of the room, making straight for the privacy of a nearby lavatory. There I fling "Tales of the Vienna Woods" into a waste basket.

Later, at home, my father is triumphant. "Didn't I tell you someday he'd be ahead of Irving Cohen? Didn't I say the whole town would be talking about him?"

"Stop saying those rotten things about Irving," I shout. "He's better than the whole bunch of you put together!"

My father and mother exchange bewildered glances.

"All of a sudden Irving Cohen is your hero?" my father asks.

I make no reply. My father and mother will never understand what has happened to me on this night. They will never understand that I have come face to face with my own cheapness, and the cheap tastes of the well-meaning audience. In shoddiness, we have been joined together, the audience and I, and I am ashamed of the union.

I exhibit my contempt for Johann Strauss, and for his devotees, and for myself, by deliberately playing "The Blue Danube Waltz" with my left hand in the key of C and my right hand in C-sharp. The dissonance is wall-crumbling.

My father is furious. "You're ruining a good piano," he cries.

"Then stop making me play this lousy Jewish music," I yell back. ("Jewish" music, according to my father, is any kind of music that has heart and soul, and into this broad category he has lumped Tchaikowsky, Chopin, Schumann, Rubinstein, and practically anybody else who has written an easily hummable tune or a melody in a minor key.)

Me at 3 years old, Sault Ste Marie, 1930

"I suppose that German anti-Semite knows what's good music, eh?" my father says derisively.

In the end I win. At my next lesson, my piano teacher shows up with two new volumes which he places ceremoniously before me at the piano — Bach's two-part inventions, and a book of Mozart's sonatas.

The days of toy music are over.

On the following Saturday, Burgess is at the door.

"I won't be going to the Algoma today," I say to him. "I'm going to Irving Cohen's house. Maybe I'll see you after the show gets out."

Burgess is off like a shot, a happy redhead bound for an afternoon with Hopalong Cassidy and Buck Rogers.

I am bound for an afternoon salon with Irving Cohen, and two composers whom I have never heard of — Debussy and George Gershwin. I have become a twelve-year-old snob.

It is 1943 and Irving Cohen and I are now two of the leading lights in the local musical world — a world that consists largely of Tony Dionisi's Dance Band ("the band that makes dyin' easy"), the Canadian Legion Fife and Drum

Corps, an assortment of teachers and musicians who frequent Anderson's Music Store to play records on Saturdays, and another assortment of teenage zoot-suited music lovers who feed the nickelodeon at Capy's Grill on Saturday nights. It is a world very much alone in space; there are no other musical planets nearby, no stars out there in the bleak universe. The town has yet to be visited by a string quartet, let alone a symphony orchestra. Solo artists – those few who dare to perform for the folks who live at the end of the railway line – are usually second-rate, on their way up to, or well on their way down from, virtuosity. The local radio station carries the Metropolitan Opera broadcasts on Saturday afternoons and the New York Philharmonic concerts on Sundays; apart from those two programs most of the air time is taken up with country-and-western and, of course, the big bands of the time – Miller, Shaw, Dorsey.

Irving is the painstaking technician, given to spending a whole afternoon at the keyboard working on a single passage until each bit of fingering has become second-nature to him. Though he remains shy and awkward in front of an audience, his technique is awesome. Under his fingers, Chopin's "Black-Keys Etude" emerges from the pianoforte like bullets from a machine gun – rapid, precise, forceful. I, on the other hand, rely on charm, plus massive applications of the loud pedal, to see me through the trickier spots. I have a kind of romantic bedside manner that lulls audiences into overlooking careless octave runs and blurred trills.

I have also become a war hero. I am one of the performers at a public concert to boost the sale of war bonds, and am in the midst of pounding out a passionate rendition of Sibelius' "Romance" when a gooseneck lamp perched atop the vibrating upright piano begins to edge forward. The lamp is irreversibly bound on a collision course with the keyboard, but I nevertheless continue playing. Precisely at the sound of the next loud base-note, the lamp plunges down, coming to rest just a few inches above the keys, where it dangles by its cord, like Damocles' sword. The audience gasps but, without missing so much as a grace note, I carry right on (those war bonds must be sold!), finishing the Romance with a dramatic flourish. Following which I rise and calmly restore the lamp to the top of the piano. The next day I am hailed in the local press as "a courageous young artist." Like Aladdin and Florence Nightingale, I have established my reputation with the aid of a lamp.

"Play us a little tune" has become a standing inside joke with Irving and me. No matter where we are, if there is a piano in the room, someone will pipe up with "Play us a little tune" and we are expected to be gracious and without further urging seat ourselves at the keyboard. There is no end to this shotgun concertizing. Furriers from Toronto, pants manufacturers from Winnipeg, dress salesmen from Montreal — it makes no difference. Each and every one is assumed to be a devotee of "good music." Singly or in groups they are corralled into the living room ("I don't care how busy you are, you must hear my son play the piano . . .") where they are obliged to sit through all three movements of a Mozart or Beethoven sonata before they can write so much as a dollar's worth of business. To a commercial traveller, whose only genuine aim is to sell his merchandise and get the hell out of Sault Ste. Marie on the next train, this mandatory musical interlude must be sheer agony. Irving and I compose special numbers for these occasions: "Prelude To The Sale of a Pair of Pants," "Overture to Overalls," "Fanfare for Furriers." There is more than a tinge of malice in this, for we are shrewd enough to sense the traveller's agony and perceptive enough to realize that he doesn't care a hoot about Mozart or Beethoven.

Given such a thin cultural atmosphere, what sustains us and helps us to flourish? It is something we have developed which I call "The Gershwin Game." Thanks to Irving's initial discovery, Irving and I have become Gershwin addicts, totally caught up in the music, the lifestyle, the wit, the lore and the legend flowing from and created around that composer. For hours at a time we play recordings of the *Rhapsody in Blue*, the *Second Rhapsody*, *Cuban Overture*, *American in Paris*, the *Three Piano Preludes*, the orchestral suite from *Porgy and Bess*, the popular show songs, and above all, the *Concerto in F*. We read and reread aloud passages from Oscar Levant's book, *A Smattering of Ignorance*, until we have memorized whole pages of dialogue between Gershwin and his friend-confidant-exponent-and-biographer. Irving takes to wearing a bar-pin through his shirt collar in the style of Gershwin and I buy my first double-breasted suit to give myself that snappy New York-in-the-Thirties look. Since Sault Ste. Marie has no Broadway, we imagine that the lights that line the canals and locks on the Michigan side of the St. Mary's River are the bright lights of the theatre district. A booth at the back of Capy's Grill becomes our Algonquin Round Table, occupied exclusively by two pseudo-sophisticates. From the other booths the uninitiated view this make-believe with a mixture of curiosity and suspicion. When the waitress brings Irving's chocolate sundae and mine, Irving points to his — which has extra whipped cream — and,

My maternal grandparents, Isaac and Norma Colish of Winnipeg (with my daughter Sarah Jane), Don Mills, 1958

With my wife, Anna Pearl, Los Angeles, 1989

borrowing a Gershwin line, says, "You see, that's the difference between genius and talent." At the end of an evening during which Irving has monopolized the keyboard at my house, I borrow a Levant line, "An evening with Irving Cohen is an Irving Cohen evening." It goes on and on and our parents and friends begin to wonder when it will end.

It ends in June, 1944. "Gershwin," who is now of draft age, joins the United States Navy. "Levant," who is not yet old enough for military service, stays behind in Sault Ste. Marie. The passion for Gershwin's music goes on. But The Gershwin Game is over. One person alone cannot play.

Twenty years have gone by. Irving Cohen has helped to win World War II off the coast of China, has finished a fine arts course at a university in Michigan, and has married. His family has left Sault Ste. Marie and I have lost track of his whereabouts and career. I am married, have two small children, and reside in the middle of a carefully planned network of cul-de-sacs and dead-end streets in a suburb of Toronto. One day the telephone rings: "Hello, it's Irving . . . Irving Cohen . . . I happen to be passing through Toronto . . . " We meet and for a few minutes The Gershwin Game is on again, revived with great enthusiasm and laughter.

At last the conversation turns to the present.

"What're you doing with yourself these days?" Irving asks.

"I'm a lawyer. What's your line?"

"Hospital linens. Sheets, pillow cases, towels. Best line in the trade. Competition can't touch our stuff for quality. We've got this new line on the market now — real soft finish, launders like a dream. A lot easier on the patients, you know; cuts down on bedsores and nuisances like that. How about you, are you specializing in anything?"

"Business law. You know — real estate, mortgages, corporate deals of various sorts. Do you still play a little piano once in a while?"

"No, not much," Irving replies. "I've changed my whole lifestyle over the years." From his jacket he withdraws a slim leather case and offers me a cigar. "Jamaican. I like 'em better than Cuban. Go ahead, take one, they're great."

Full-cheeked and thick-lipped, like two contented bullfrogs, we sit blowing thick clouds of cigar smoke into the air. "Did you read recently that George Gershwin suffered from chronic constipation all during his adult life, and that he visited brothels from time to time?" I ask.

"You're kidding?" Irving responds, smiling incredulously.

"Honest-to-God."

"Too bad about Levant," he says, snapping his gold cigar clipper open and shut. "He sure turned into a wreck. I saw him try to play part of the slow movement of Gershwin's *Concerto in F* one night on Jack Paar's show. What a disaster!"

"I guess you and I were smart to stay out of the music business."

We nod in agreement. Two men who made the right decisions years ago, each at his own point somewhere along the path that leads from genius to talent, and from talent to reality.

*The Ungerman family in 1931. Had the elder Ungermans been alive today, they could boast 94 descendents.
(Back row, left to right: Jack, age 18; Harry, age 19. Middle Row, left to right: Betty, age 15; my mother, Jennie,
age 36; my father, Isaac, age 37; David, age 16. Front row, left to right: Karl, age 7; Ida, age 10; Irving, age 9)*

IRVING UNGERMAN

───── ✥ ─────

Fighting My Way Up

My parents, Isaac and Jennie Ungerman, were both born in the town of Bogria, Poland. They married in 1911, at the young ages of twenty and seventeen, and emigrated to Canada three years later with their first two sons, Harry and Jack. My father passed away early, of a stroke in 1954 at age sixty-three. My mother, the matriarch of our family, survived him by nearly thirty years, passing away in 1983.

After arriving in Toronto, my parents moved flats several times until they settled on Cecil Street. My dad got a job at a kosher meat abattoir, where he worked twenty-hour days. During those years on Cecil Street, three more children arrived: David and Betty (both now in their eighties), and Ida, who lived until 1990.

After struggling to support five children on a wage of ten dollars a week, my parents moved to 38 Kensington Avenue to open their very own kosher butcher shop. That is where I was born, on February 1, 1923. Then the baby of the family, Karl (known as Kievy), came along in May of the following year. Both my parents were great humanitarians and could not stand to see any family go without food. They never hesitated to extend credit to customers, a natural generosity that eventually pushed them into bankruptcy.

My Bar Mitzvah photo, 1936

Brothers Karl, age 3, and Irving, age 4, in 1927

The family continued to live on Kensington until 1934, when we moved to 216 Royce Avenue, now known as Dupont Street. Moving day was February 1, my eleventh birthday. That date looms in my memory as the turning point in our family fortunes, when success began to come our way. After that winter day in 1934, I always chose to make important decisions and life changes on my birthday. In addition, those classic lucky numerals "7-11" became my favourite numbers. Even today they can be found on my vehicle licence plates and wherever else I can use them.

During the decade from 1927 to '37, my maternal grandparents, Zaida Hershel Sopman and Bubby Pearl, owned a hundred-acre farm at Scarlett Road and Eglinton Avenue. We all spent the summers there, learning to milk the cows, churn butter and cheese, and swim in the Humber River. It was a sad day when my Zaida was forced to sell that large piece of farmland for a mere $8,000. Try as he might, he was unable to secure his children's and grandchildren's futures as we can today.

When we moved from Kensington Avenue in 1934, my parents were financially depleted from extending credit to people even poorer than ourselves. Our family was forced to live within severely restricted means; we faced serious hardships, with triple mortgages on a building worth only $7,000. We were no longer operating any specific type of business. Instead, my father became a pedlar of scrap and chickens, a man desperately trying to keep his family clothed and fed and warm. All of the seven children were called upon to help. Harry was selling newspapers at the corner of King and Yonge streets. Jack was delivering CN telegrams by bicycle. And Dave was working for the *Toronto Telegram*, tossing bundles of newspapers from the back of a truck onto various city corners.

Two years after moving to Royce Avenue, my father's experience peddling chickens led him to the conclusion that people in the neighbourhood wished to purchase live chickens. And so was born Royce Avenue Poultry and Egg Market. When Royce Avenue became Dupont Street, we changed the store's name to Royce Dupont Poultry Packers.

When I turned thirteen, I was bar mitzvahed at the Junction's Maria Street Shul, which still exists and is today designated a historic building. That year I got a job as a drugstore delivery boy. I worked six days from 4 to 10 P.M., earning the grand total of $2.50 per week — two dollars of which I immediately handed over to my mother. I was able to save fifty cents a week, just enough to pay my dues to the Central YMCA. Barely a teenager, I was determined to learn how to protect myself from the tough anti-Semites in the neighbourhood. They would paint swastikas on our store windows, call out hateful names and threaten us. Right next door to our building there was a pool hall that attracted the roughest and the toughest types, such as members of the notorious Polka Dot Gang.

These humiliations carried over into the schoolyard and classroom corridors. I remember one young boy in particular who unleashed the ugliest insults because I was Jewish. Although I had by that time only a little experience with boxing, my instinct for self-defence led me to beat him up, hitting him from pillar to post right there in the cloakroom, and causing him to bleed from various head cuts. Naturally, I was suspended from school and given a strapping, which only strengthened my resolve to fight and intensified my interest in boxing. I began to enter many competitions, and by age sixteen I won the Newsboy's City Boxing Championship — weighing a mere 105 pounds!

During my teen years, I trained and fought at a number of gyms, including Foresters Hall, the YMCA, and Elm Grove. With ringside admission prices as low as one dollar, I also managed to attend many of the boxing matches held at Oakwood Stadium, Sunnyside's Palace Pier, Massey Hall, Mutual Street Arena, and Maple Leaf Gardens. I saw fights featuring Dave Castello,

In front of the Royce Avenue store in 1939

Above: My parents, Jennie and Isaac, c. 1940
Right: Jennie Ungerman, 1941

Henry Hook, Spider Armstrong, and Jackie Callura. I was in the stands for Steve Rocco, the Bagnatos, Arthur King, Georgie Pace, Indian Quintena, and Earl Walls — to name just a few. I also closely followed the careers of Toronto's early Jewish fighters. Those names are with me like it was yesterday: Sam Goodman, who fought as early as 1915, Sammy Luftspring, Baby Yack, Norm Hurdman, Max Kadin, Dave Peters, and Al Grace. Then there was Montreal's Max Berger, and the American one-legged boxer, Tommy Spiegel. And I could never forget the boxing referee Harry Davis, who is refereeing to this day.

In addition to my passion for boxing, I invested much energy in the family business from the time I was sixteen to nineteen. My two oldest brothers, Harry and Jack, went on to set up their own poultry plant partnership called Toronto Packing. That left Dave, Betty and her husband Moe, Ida and her husband Manny, Karl, and myself, to help our father and mother build a successful poultry processing business. My role included driving

122

From left to right, Karl, Irving, David, Jack, and Harry, 1941

a truck, making deliveries, doing bookkeeping and sales — whatever it took to fill a sixteen-hour workday. I had just completed Grade 8 as a top student, but my formal education was nonetheless now a thing of the past.

At nineteen, I was eligible to apply to the Armed Services, and so I joined the Royal Canadian Air Force (RCAF). My parents hung up a flag with five stars, one for each son in the Canadian Forces. This by no means marked an end to my life in the ring, as I immediately began to fight in boxing matches against the army and navy. I won many RCAF trophies and silver spoons for my efforts. When I was transferred from the Manning Depot in Toronto to Halifax's Y Depot, I went on to beat members of the various forces stationed there. It was also my good fortune to rediscover in Halifax one of my first boxing coaches at the Toronto YMCA, Cosmo Conzano. He was now a flight sergeant, but still let me greet him as my "coach"! In September 1942, I was shipped to England, where I eagerly continued boxing against other branches of the military.

Our group was still based in England when D-Day preparations were underway in the spring of 1944. I could never have known, one fateful day out on the firing range with my contingent, that the D-Day order was only twenty-four hours away. During the shooting exercise I was hit accidentally by a bullet from someone else's sten gun. That bullet went right through my forearm, causing an injury that put me in hospital and prevented me from participating

NG TELEGRAM, TORONTO, TUESDAY, OCTOBER 3, 1944

Toronto Family Proud Of Its Sons

DAVID UNGERMAN   IRVING UNGERMAN   KARL UNGERMAN   JACK UNGERMAN

Mr. and Mrs. Isaac Ungerman, 216 Royce ave., are justly proud of their four sons on active service in the army and air force. Flying Officer David Ungerman, 29, recently completed a tour of operations as an RCAF air-bomber; Irving, 21, is a corporal in the air force in England; Karl, 20, is taking a pilot's course in the RCAF and is now stationed at No. 1 ITS, Eglinton; Jack, 21, is stationed at Camp Borden in the Army Service Corps. A fifth son, Harry, 32, was in the army for a short time but was later discharged because of a leg injury.

*From the Toronto Evening
Telegram, October 3, 1944*

in the D-Day invasion. How ironic that this stray bullet meant I would not become one of the many D-Day casualties suffered by my contingent. Hearing all the guns and aircraft overhead as I lay in my hospital bed suddenly made me realize that my remaining alive was *beshert*; it was simply meant to be. I still recall with gratitude the welcome visits within a few days of the invasion from Canadian army chaplain Rabbi David Monson, and my RCAF chaplain Rabbi Jacob Eisen. During my rehabilitation eight months later, I was given an Honourable Medical Discharge and sent home.

It was 1945 when I returned from overseas and rededicated myself to further developing our family business. That same year, a Mrs. Chuvalo worked at our plant, hand-plucking individual chickens for two and a half cents per bird, which earned her about thirty dollars a week. My father would babysit the Chuvalos' four-year-old son, George, while his mother was working. It is funny to think back on that early connection to the Chuvalo family at a time when nobody could predict that our futures would one day be linked.

After my medical discharge, I visited New York City, where I met Sylvia Rothstein of Rockaway Beach, Long Island. Within a year we were married. During those early years of our long and lucky marriage (fifty years and counting!), I worked endless hours with my father, brother Karl, and brother-in-law Manny. As well as the hard work, a series of successful investments such as purchasing lands and farms helped the business to grow quickly. We produced

250,000 turkeys a year, plus our chicken requirement. We processed that volume and then sold it wholesale and in our retail store.

In 1958 an eighteen-year-old George Chuvalo reignited my love of boxing when I witnessed him fighting in the Jack Dempsey Heavyweight Tournaments. His mother, aunt, and uncle were still working in our plant during this period, and in 1962 they quite unexpectedly approached me with a request to be his manager. That launched my second career: the management and promotion of boxing throughout the world. Chuvalo became Canada's undefeated heavyweight champion and has a record of 97 fights without ever being knocked off his feet. During his boxing career he took on legendary fighters such as Floyd Patterson, Joe Frazier, Muhammad Ali (twice), and George Foreman. He also fought a host of others, including Buster Mathis, Jerry Quarry, Dante Cane, Manuel Ramos, and Doug Jones. Chuvalo's career with me lasted until his retirement in the 1980s.

During these years my management and promotions extended across international borders. Clients included both Canadian and Commonwealth welterweight champs Clyde Gray and Donovan Boucher; the British middleweight champion Roy Gumbs; as well as the Summerhays brothers, Nicky Furlano, Eddie Melo, and Remo Decarlo. How exciting it was for me, a young Jewish man, to have personal contact with boxing's greats: Jack Dempsey, Jack Sharkey, Barney Ross, Max Baer, Joe Louis, Rocky Marciano, Muhammad Ali, Sugar Ray Leonard, Marvin Hagler, Jake La Motta, and Willy Pep. The illustrious list takes in the dealmakers and promoters, like Bob Arum (who became my close friend), Don King, Teddy Brenner of Madison Square Gardens, Harry Levine, and Mickey Duff of London, England. In 1963, I was instrumental in introducing closed-circuit television to Canada with the George Chuvalo – Floyd Patterson fight. Closed-circuit TV was to become a major component of my fight promotions.

Meanwhile, our business flourished. In 1987 we built a new, state-of-the-art, fully automated processing plant. It was then that Maple Leaf Foods approached us to buy the business, asking me to stay on as CEO for five years. And so, after sixty years of operating Royce Dupont Poultry, my brother, Karl, and I sold the Ungerman interest to Maple Leaf in 1988. I was sixty-five then, and continued to work full time until I began my retirement at age seventy. We have still retained a retail outlet on Dupont Street known as Royce Dupont Farms.

Studying film of Muhammad Ali in preparation for George Chuvalo's fight against him, Maple Leaf Gardens, March 29, 1966 (left to right: Rocky Marciano, Joe Louis, George Chuvalo, and Irving Ungerman)

On top of all our good fortune, for Sylvia and me our proudest achievement is our three children – Shelley, Howard, and Temmi – all with professional careers, who have given us seven grandchildren spread over more than two decades! Once again, my lucky number shows up in my total number of grandchildren. I often remember my parents, generous and charitable people, who tried to instill these values in their children. I, in turn, have tried to show a similar example to mine. I recall my parents donating two Sefer Torahs to the Beth Sholom Synagogue when it was a new congregation, as well as a large stained-glass window of a Chanukah scene. My eldest daughter was the first baby to be named there in 1947, and Sylvia and I have continued the family tradition by donating works of art to the synagogue and establishing the Ungerman Museum, which displays Jewish artifacts that date back several hundred years. Sylvia has also served as president of the Sisterhood, and I, too, have served on the Board of Governors of the synagogue for many years and still remain active.

Our love of Jewish values has led to involvement in groups whose development is intertwined with the growth of Toronto's Jewish community – from Mount Sinai Hospital to Baycrest Centre, the Shaarezedec Hospital, and the Reena Foundation. But my humble roots and belief in this city's potential have also kept me faithful to such broader community institutions as the Salvation Army and the Variety Club, and I am a founding director of the Santa Claus Parade.

The Ungerman family in 1989
(Back row, left to right: Karl, age 65;
Irving, age 66; David, age 74; Jack, age 75;
Harry, age 76. Front row, left to right:
Ida, age 67, now deceased; Betty, age 72)

Fittingly, everything has come full circle in the sphere of Jewish athletics. For the past twenty-eight years, as the past Canadian fundraising chairman of the Maccabi Games, I have travelled to Israel with the Canadian team every four years, for a total of seven visits. I was the first Jewish person to be elected into the Canadian Boxing Hall of Fame and the first Canadian to have been inducted into the Maccabi International Jewish Hall of Fame in Israel.

Like others in Toronto's Jewish community who were lucky enough to prosper in what was for their parents an adopted land, we were able to build a cottage in Muskoka that has been a constant in our lives since 1957 – a haven amid all the ups and downs. When I think of my parents' shtetl in Poland, of my birth on Kensington Avenue and my various moves, I ultimately come back to my cottage of forty years. Today, as I reflect upon the diverse experiences and accomplishments in my life, it is from this beautiful vantage point in the Canadian countryside that I savour my fondest memories.

At Tel Asher, north of Tel Aviv, 1930, armed to deal with Arab intruders

Zionism in the Family

I was seven years old when a single incident taught me firsthand what it meant to be a Jew. Our parents had told us about the anti-Jewish pogroms that had marked the Russian civil war. My mother, always a tireless charity worker, was seeking homes for the children orphaned by those massacres, and my parents had volunteered to add one of them to our own family. So on a cold, grey, rainy day at our lakeside cottage north of Toronto, my brother Joe and I, and my sisters Zelda and Ronny, huddled outside, waiting.

Our long, soggy wait came to an end as Mother and Dad drove up and we swarmed excitedly around the car. Then we fell back, awed into silence, as my mother helped out a pale, utterly silent figure, his pinched face dominated by a pair of dark and remote black eyes.

When she had settled Ernie into his room, Mother took us aside and tried to explain what had happened to Ernie to put him in this state. His parents had been killed before his eyes, and then he had been separated from the rest of his family and sent halfway around the world to complete strangers. He was still, she explained, in a state of shock.

So, to a lesser degree, were we. The little boy about my age who lay on his bed for hours on end with his face to the wall, ignoring our friendly advances,

Our family, beneath Mother's watchful eye (clockwise, from bottom left: Ronny, Joe, me, Zelda, Ernie)

was a striking lesson to us. In a very real sense, Ernie's suffering brought home what it meant to be a Jew in other parts of the world. The lesson learned in the two or three weeks that it took Ernie to "thaw out" and become a full member of our family, to our lasting delight and benefit, was one I will never forget.

The episode also reinforced my love for Ernie's new home – Canada. At the same time, growing up Jewish in Toronto was for me synonymous with growing up a Zionist. I am a Canadian and a Jew, with strong loyalties to both Canada and Israel – loyalties which have shaped my life, and will to my last day.

Our family – the one Ernie joined – was a very happy one and a very affluent one. My childhood home was a rambling, English-style mansion, set on a ninety-acre estate known as Sunnybrook Farm, located just off Bayview Avenue, near what is now Sunnybrook Hospital. It was a very large house, with five storeys of living space, servants' quarters, a library, and a big, airy morning room. Despite its size, it was warm and cosy and had a lived-in feeling. For us children, it was a dreamland. Off the oaken bar was a secret panel leading to a tunnel that wound under the potting sheds to a thickly wooded ravine below. There was plenty of space to explore and hunt and play and roam; and it was Sunnybrook, I believe, that gave me a lifelong love of the outdoors.

Our wealth was due to my father David's business success, a rags-to-riches story that would have made Horatio Alger proud. He was a poor immigrant from Macover, Poland, who went bankrupt in New York selling shoes on credit – then a revolutionary idea, but typical of my father's daring approach to retail business. Later, when the family moved to Toronto, Dad went to work for his father, Elias, making buttonholes for clothing manufacturers. It was Dad's job to pick up the garments to be serviced, using a horse and wagon. He thus managed to save up the then princely sum of $1,500 and started his own wholesale suit company, with his main retail store on Yonge Street.

At first, business was bad, but he conceived the original idea of selling tailor-made suits at a single price – fourteen dollars – and offered a twenty-five-dollar prize to the person who came up with the catchiest name for the store. A local journalist won, and Tip Top Tailors was born. Twenty of the single-priced suits sold the first day, and my father never looked back. Tip Top would grow into Canada's largest clothing chain, with sixty-five stores across the country. Following his death, my father was inducted into the Canadian Business Hall of Fame.

While I lacked for nothing growing up in Toronto, at private school my academic career was, to put it modestly, not stellar. It was on the playing field where I came into my own. I played hockey and football with great zest, and because I had become unusually big and strong, with plenty of stamina, I was able to play through an entire football game without being relieved. "Stop Dunkelman!" became the chief defensive tactic of any school that played against us.

Perhaps it was because of my size, but I never encountered any overt anti-Semitism as a boy, in school or elsewhere. I had an absolutely carefree youth, playing all manner of sports during the school year, and sailing, swimming, and fishing on nearby Lake Simcoe during the idyllic summers. I might have turned into a spoiled young playboy, except that my mother, Rose, would never have stood for it.

Rose Miller had been the daughter of one of my father's suppliers in the early days, and she and Dad were wed in 1910. Later, when he had the means, my father became one of the largest local contributors to Jewish and Zionist causes. Mother, though, was an even more dedicated champion of Zionism, a whirlwind of energy and communal work, and a woman of great passion. While her energies were mostly directed toward Jewish charities, she was also an officer of the Canadian Red Cross, where her humanitarian efforts earned her the Coronation Medal in 1937.

With encouragement from my father, Mother made our home a transit station and hospitality centre for Zionist leaders who were in Toronto to address meetings or seek help for a project. Her salon came to be known as "The Canadian Zionist Embassy." I would sit enthraled, listening to the visitors' accounts of exotic Palestine. One speaker particularly impressed me. He had just returned from South Africa and had visited a game reserve there. "Although the world has set aside land for animals," he rued, "they quibble over a land for the Jews."

The man was Chaim Weizmann, later to become Israel's first President, and at the time head of the World Zionist Organization, travelling around the world to ignite Zionist ardour and seek *chalutzim* (pioneers). I was most profoundly stirred, however, when Weizmann spoke of the hundreds of thousands of Jews already pioneering in Palestine. They were planting the groves, draining the swamps, and tending the long-neglected soil, all while defending themselves against hostile Arabs ringing their tiny communities. His words held me spellbound. So I became increasingly determined to visit Palestine one day.

Young Dunkelman, in his Upper Canada College blazer, armed to deal with quarrelsome playmates

I didn't have long to wait. In 1930, as my seventeenth birthday approached, my parents presented me with a return ticket to Palestine and $500 spending money. I eagerly accepted and turned a vacation into a one-year stay.

As our train from Alexandria approached Jerusalem, I was gripped with excitement and anticipation. There I was, following the route trudged by Moses and the Children of Israel. The antiquated train chugged through the Judean hills, and a great sense of contentment, of continuity with my ancestors, and of peace washed over me. It was the feeling of a returning exile.

That feeling remained, even during the hardships of being an orange-grove worker and watchman at Tel Asher, a small, windswept settlement north of Tel Aviv. There, I endured the backbreaking toil of having to stoop to hoe the hard, red earth, leaving my muscles in torment and my palms a mass of raw flesh; the sleep deprivation caused by straw mattresses infested with venomous insects; the sparse food; the tension of keeping watch against Arab marauders, equipped only with an old shotgun and my training as a boxer and wrestler, which I used in at least one successful hand-to-hand battle with an Arab even bigger than I was. For all this, I was paid twenty piastres (one dollar) a day — enough so that six months later I could afford to buy a donkey.

Yet it was all so exhilarating.

Once I proved I could put in a hard day's work, I was accepted; no longer was I the soft outsider. My friends at Tel Asher were hell-raisers. After sweating under an unbearable sun all day, we would gladly dance half the night away. I became intoxicated by the land and its people, who were unlike any Jews I'd known — proud, uncompromising, bowing their heads before no one.

The soft, pampered kid who left Toronto a year before, returned a toughened, lean nineteen-year-old, ready to make his mark at Tip Top Tailors by helping his father through the Great Depression. My intention, however, was always to return to Palestine to live one day.

My authority in the company grew as the years passed. I was able to introduce new merchandising ideas, a ladies' wear department, and other initiatives that helped turn the company around, enabling it to make a profit after several losing years. My love for the creativity involved in the garment trade grew.

At the same time, my concern for the increasingly persecuted Jews of Europe likewise grew, and I devoted myself, as my mother had, to the Zionist movement and fundraising on behalf of Youth Aliya. And when Canada declared war on Germany in 1939, I announced my plans to sign up for armed service.

The Dinny, *my topsail schooner designed by Hand, speeds across Georgian Bay with me at the helm*

Father, Ronny, Zelda, and B.D. strolling on the boardwalk at Atlantic City in 1936

Volunteer? My parents said I was crazy to brush aside my exempt status. Didn't I know I was in an essential war industry? Look at your plans, they said, to set up a Tip Top plant capable of cranking out 35,000 uniforms a week. The whole idea of signing up was the height of irresponsibility! My father had even succeeded in arranging an offer from the Ordnance Corps to put me in charge of supply procurement, with the rank of Brigadier.

I turned it all down. I wanted to join a fighting unit.

I don't want to dwell on my experiences during World War II; they are well summarized in my autobiography *Dual Allegiance*. Like millions of other Allied soldiers, we fought the Nazis, as members of the Queen's Own Rifles of Canada, in France, Belgium, the Netherlands, and Germany. I rose from Rifleman to Major, commanded a rifle company, and won the Distinguished Service Order.

Second Lieutenant Ben Dunkelman of the Queen's Own Rifles of Canada

The battle for Mooshof in February 1945, eight months after the Allied forces landed on D-Day, stands out in my mind as the most difficult and trying operation up to that time.

We were the first Allied troops to take up and hold positions on the Rhine river where it joins the Neder Rijn. Now, the orders for Operation Blockbuster came. We were to drive the Germans back from their famed Schlieffen Line. Previous Allied attacks on Mooshof had been repulsed by a crack, tenacious enemy. This time, the enemy had been softened up by heavy air and artillery bombardment. Then it was our turn – D Company's. With three platoons, we overcame light resistance and reached our objective – the farm buildings of Mooshof. Not a single casualty.

Then all hell broke loose. The enemy's defensive tactics were brilliantly conceived. Under attack, they had held on as long as possible in their excellently concealed slit-trenches, then had withdrawn to prepared positions a little farther back, allowing their opponents to advance. Their previously ranged mortar and artillery fire was poured onto the positions they'd just vacated, sacrificing a few of their own men still there. And co-ordinated with the deadly accurate shelling was an infantry assault to retake the ground they'd just left. Superb tactics.

One of our platoons was in the crossfire; members of another came to the rescue and were soon caught in the same deadly rain of bombs and bullets. All around me, men were being killed and wounded, men I had lived with and led and trusted for three months. And now there was nothing I could do but help carry their bodies to cover and try to look after the wounded.

We returned fire, and the battle swayed back and forth, attack and counter-attack. In the end we won the position simply by wearing the enemy down. But it was a Pyrrhic victory. At the end of that gruesome day, there were only 36 fighting men left in my company, out of the 115 who started. I was the only officer to come through unwounded, along with only one NCO.

As for the Distinguished Service Order, it was awarded to me after I figured out a way to get my men through the mine-strewn Hochwald forest: by leaping from the base of one tree to the next and clinging to the trunks, since we reasoned (correctly) that no one would go to the lengths of planting a mine underneath a large tree root.

My war-time experiences made news back home. The federal Liberals offered me a safe parliamentary seat in the heavily Jewish riding of Spadina in the election of 1945. An MP's job was mine for the asking, with the possibility of a cabinet post to follow, most likely the labour portfolio. But I turned it down to stay at the front after a delegation of my men from D Company implored, "Don't leave us, sir. If you go, we'll all be dead before long." I was flattered by the genuine devotion shown by these battle-hardened troops.

Another far-off war beckoned in 1948, and I felt obliged to volunteer. The new-born State of Israel seemed doomed to die before it could even crawl. Its raw, ill-trained army was hopelessly outnumbered by the joint forces of a half-dozen Arab countries. The Israeli "tanks" were actually ordinary Dodge trucks with metal welded to their chassis. Mortars were made of sewer pipe.

Even before the British pulled their troops out of Palestine, I had been serving as Canadian chairman of the Hagana, the underground Jewish organization that recruited some thousand of us Canadian volunteers to join Jewish fighters in Palestine — more than from any other country. I became the first member of the Machal (foreign volunteers) to sneak through the blockade imposed by my erstwhile British comrades-in-arms. To get around British immigration restrictions on Jews, I sailed from Marseilles to Haifa with a forged passport, and tried — mainly in vain — to affect the British accent of its bearer, a "Mr. Fox" from Twickenham.

My immediate superior upon my arrival was a tall, handsome lad with a fair complexion and blue eyes. At twenty-six, he was the youngest brigade commander in the Israeli forces. He was Yitzhak Rabin, later to serve two terms as prime minister and be felled by an assassin's bullet for his daring peace initiatives. "We Jews have a secret weapon in our struggle with the Arabs," Rabin once told me. "We have no other place to go."

I started as his assistant planning officer. Rabin's orders were to reopen the road from the coastal plain and relieve the Arab siege of Jerusalem. Soon he handed me the authority to open the road, using the knowledge I had picked up in the Queen's Own. Employing mortar over impossible terrain and repulsing counter-attacks, we retook the entire thirty-mile strip, bypassing the Arab garrison at Latrun that had prevented supplies from reaching Jerusalem from Tel Aviv. The stretch was later paved and renamed The Road of Valour. Until the 1967 war, it remained the only artery connecting Tel Aviv to Jerusalem. I had Rabin to thank for my success, and Amos Horev, a brave fighter, who went on to head the world-famous Technion in Haifa, and Menachem and his battalion from Yitzhak's Harel brigade.

In Israel, 1948

Rabin responded by writing the foreword to *Dual Allegiance*, and he remained a great, true friend to his last day.

I will never forget my first meeting with the fledgling state's top commander and first prime minister. David Ben-Gurion expressed a keen personal interest in me, firing one question after another at me about my background. In time, he came to trust me — a trust likely based on the practical military know-how I had acquired during World War II — and soon he ordered that I be granted access to him day or night.

At the time, the Jews of Palestine manufactured their own six-inch mortars. These were very primitive weapons, and in fact the Ordnance Corps refused to approve them. Ben-Gurion gave me the unprecedented authority to give orders to anyone in civilian production or the army in an attempt to see if we could successfully put them into production. I quickly proved these mortars could be handled safely and effectively, and they were soon put to use. He also put me in command of the heavy mortar brigade.

I had hoped to return to Jerusalem on the very road we had just freed, but instead, Ben-Gurion appointed me commander of the Armored 7th Brigade. My orders were to move the brigade north, and we were given just seven days to reorganize the unit and take over the defence of the western coastal plains bordering the Mediterranean from just south of Acre to Rusell Nakoura on the Lebanese border to the north.

The Arab army of liberation, under the command of Fawzi-el-Kauji, was holding the foothills to the east overlooking our positions in the plains below. They were very active, and we were under constant attack over the entire front. We immediately started to counter-attack the most important positions that Kauji had established, and were successful in taking them over, denying them their vantage points.

We then mounted an attack on Nazareth. After its conquest, we controlled all the foothills to the north and south. This allowed us to manoeuvre our troops out of sight of the enemy and make a surprise attack from Safed in the east while drawing a great deal of our strength from the west.

Some time later, when I had returned to my headquarters in Acre for a few hours of rest, I was about to sink into bed when my driver appeared. "*Adon Ben!*" ("Ben, sir!"), he cried. Angrily, I asked him what he wanted. He said there was a messenger outside with a dispatch from Northern Command in Nazareth.

"Well, why don't you take it?" I growled.

"She won't give it to anyone but you or your second-in-command, and he's not around."

I flung on some clothes and stormed into the courtyard. I was pleasantly surprised to encounter a slender girl with long, wavy black hair, large hazel eyes, in a neat brown cotton uniform. I snatched the envelope from her hand, spun on my heels, and returned to my quarters.

As I climbed the stairs, my anger subsided sufficiently for me to think. I had been miserable toward that girl and made a mental note to apologize to her should we meet again.

The envelope contained a top-secret order to report to divison HQ in Nazareth the following day. In Nazareth I discovered that the attractive messenger was Yael Lifshitz, the daughter of David Lifshitz, a prominent engineer who had helped found the Palestine Electric Corporation. Not long after, I did apologize, and invited her to lunch. By the time the meal was over, I was smitten. A month later I proposed marriage, and have remained smitten for nearly half a century.

At the meeting at division HQ, Moshe Carmel, the commander of the north, gave me orders to proceed with the attack in the north of Israel using the plan I had prepared. The operation was to be called Hiram, and all the troops in the field were to be under my command.

We had to move our entire brigade to our starting point on the outskirts of Safad at night, in the blackout, and with complete silence through some very difficult terrain. It would be essential to keep the entire brigade under cover. The engineers, working throughout the night, had cleared the mines and obstacles from the road without alerting the enemy so that at dawn on the next day we could dash west down the road, secure our flank at Meron, and rush north to capture Sasa, the first key objective of our operation. We ended up reaching as far north as the Litani river in Lebanon, from where we eventually withdrew. Today, a bridge across Israel's Northern Road, which skirts the Lebanese border, is named Ben's Bridge.

B.H. Liddell Hart, the famous military tactician has a description of this attack in the revised edition of his book *Strategy*.* This book is recognised as a

*B.H. Liddel Hart, *Strategy*, 2nd revd ed. (New York: Meridian, 1991), pp. 402-405. A full account of this operation can be found in Ben Dunkelman, *Dual Allegiance* (Toronto: Macmillan Company of Canada, 1976), pp. 288-97.

Yael Lifshitz

A detail of our wedding photo. Sitting next to Yael is Ya'acov Dori, then Israel's Chief-of-Staff, and in front of me is Yael's brother, Avigdor.

On Israel's Northern Road, skirting the Lebanese border. The sign reads, "Gesher Ben" ("Ben's Bridge"). On the right is Hoter Ishai, 7th Brigade's DAQMG

David Ben-Gurion, first Prime Minister of Israel. The Hebrew inscription reads, "To Ben Dunkelman, the commander of the Israeli forces who had the privilege of participating in the conquest of Galilee. With thanks, Ben-Gurion."

classic on military strategy. Its author is one of the world's foremost military thinkers — a man generally regarded as the "von Clausewitz of the twentieth century."

Shortly after our victory in Hiram, Yael and I were married on the top of Mount Carmel in her family home in Haifa. Several weeks later, we had another grand wedding celebration with the Druze in the western Galilee with hundreds of people in attendance. Ben-Gurion had phoned to say that he could not attend because of a cabinet meeting and sent us the following telegram the next day: "To Benjamin Ben David [my Israeli name] and his bride: Sincere congratulations on the occasion of their marriage. Instead of the wedding gift we are accustomed to give to the bridegroom, the bridegroom has brought a present to the Jewish nation — the freedom of Galilee. And together with his soldiers and all the people of Israel, I congratulate him and his bride and wish them a happy life. Victory and peace, [signed] D. Ben-Gurion."

When the war was over, Ben-Gurion offered me a supreme military honour: the peacetime job of commanding the entire Israeli armoured corps, with the very real possibility of eventually becoming Chief-of-Staff. I suggested I could be of more service by joining his efforts to provide food and housing for the stream of immigrants who had entered the country and who continued to arrive in enormous numbers.

In 1974, Prime Minister Yitzhak Rabin greets Yael and me in Jerusalem

Shortly after, Yael and I left Israel – temporarily, we thought – when my mother took deathly ill in Toronto. Not much later, she died. My father was ready to retire, and became adamant that I should take over the business. Although Yael and I had meant to return to Israel permanently, and more than once came very close to doing so, events would always seem to conspire against us.

Like the Spanish philosopher Judah ha-Levi, I am in the West, but my heart will always be in Israel.

PART THREE

MY ZAIDA'S LEGACY

Joey and Harold Tanenbaum as young boys

My Zaida's Legacy

On my graduation from University of Toronto with a degree in civil engineering, age 22

My late beloved grandfather Abraham Tanenbaum arrived in Toronto in August of 1911 with only eight dollars in his pocket. The way he told it, on board the ship from Hamburg to New York, he met two *landsmen*, two men from his own village of Parczew, in Poland. When he asked them where they were going, they said, "To Toronto." My Zaida enquired if Toronto was in America. When they replied positively, he said, "Then I will go with you."

The three travellers arrived at 2 P.M. on a Friday afternoon, just before the Sabbath, at the southwest corner of St. Clair Avenue and Runnymede Road. This was where the trains came in. The place was called The Junction, because it was where all the rail traffic to Toronto from the east, the west, and the north converged.

Because my Zaida was much more observant than his companions, he decided that he would stay in the area and try to find a Jewish home with a *mezuzah* where he could spend the Sabbath. After that, he thought, he would proceed on Sunday to the Spadina and College Street area, where he knew there was a Jewish community.

Fortunately for our family, one block south of St. Clair and just east of Runnymede Road was — and still is — Maria Street. There my Zaida found a small, thriving enclave of immigrant Jews. He was so enchanted with the place, he didn't just spend the weekend; he decided to settle down on Maria Street, and made his home there for the next forty years.

My Zaida started out as a pedlar with a pushcart. After three years, he had saved enough money to bring my beloved Bubbie (my grandmother) and their two children — eight-year-old Joe and five-year-old Max — to Canada. They arrived on August 3, 1914, the very same day that the British Empire declared war on Germany and the First World War began for Canada.

Then my two aunts were born — Aunty Sara Katz, in 1915, and Aunty Esther Gottlieb, in 1917 — the first members of our family to be born in Canada.

By 1917 Zaida was able to buy his first *ferdele*, his first horse. He would tell me in Yiddish, "*Yoselebein es hast gewesen the shoenste ferdele in the ganze weld*," that it was the most beautiful horse in the whole world. Both my dad and my uncle Joe would say, "It was the ugliest beast you ever saw!" Which proves that beauty is in the eye of the beholder!

Now that my Zaida had a horse and wagon, he needed a piece of land to store all of his used material. He was able to purchase the northwest corner of Runnymede and Dundas Street — three hundred feet west on Dundas and five hundred feet north on Runnymede — for $200 in cash and an $1,800 first mortgage at 3 per cent. The man who gave Zaida the mortgage was none other than Herb Solway's late grandfather.

Within four years — that is, in 1921 — a real-estate agent came to Zaida to purchase part of the corner, sixty feet by sixty feet. Zaida would tell me how he sold the piece of land for $16,000 cash to the Toronto Railway Commission, which today is the TTC. But the *Mail*, the predecessor of the *Globe and Mail*, reported that Abraham Tanenbaum had sold the corner of Runnymede and Dundas, to be used as the most westerly turning-point for Toronto's streetcars, for the princely sum of $96,000.

Purely a *typographical* error!

Zaida told me the banks came to him and said, "Mr. Tanenbaum, anything you want, you can have." Zaida's reply was, "I'll give you $16,000 now and the other $80,000 at a later date, provided you're good to me." In August of 1942, he told me that the bank was still waiting for the other $80,000!

The Year of the Horse, 1917, marked the beginning of Runnymede Metal & Salvage Company. It also saw the first of the sacrifices that the second generation would make for the future of our family. On December 11 of that year, Zaida

My father, Max's, Bar Mitzvah photo, 1922 (left to right: aunt Sara Katz, age 7; Bubbie Chira, age 38; uncle Joe, age 16; aunt Esther Gottlieb, age 4; Zaida Abraham, age 45; father Max, age 13)

took Uncle Joe out of Grade 6 to help with the fledgling business. Uncle Joe's role was initially to look after the employees in the yard and later to manage the wrecking of the buildings and bridges that would be demolished by Runnymede.

My father, Max, had it a bit "easier." He stayed in Annette Street public school until he completed Grade 8! Dad would tell the story of how he celebrated his Bar Mitzvah on June 28, 1922, and how, on the following Monday, Zaida took him into the business as well. Dad's first job, at the tender age of thirteen, was to deal with the banks.

In fact I still have hanging in my office the original balance sheet that my dad prepared on July 18, 1924. It shows that the family assets, less the liabilities, came to the grand total of $21,722.78.

By 1928 the foundations of the family business were laid. Zaida and his sons purchased the complete structural steel inventory of Reid & Brown, which had gone bankrupt that year. This purchase catapulted what was now Runnymede Iron & Steel Company into the steel fabricating business. By the outbreak of World War II, Runnymede was the second-largest fabricator in the City of Toronto, next to Dominion Bridge.

What my Zaida taught his sons about business, he handed down to me as well. He imparted to me his wisdom and his principles. What he gave me was a philosophy of life.

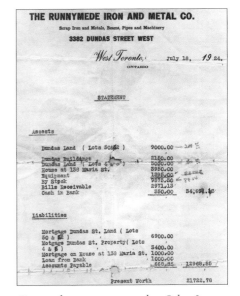

Financial statement prepared on July 18, 1924, by my late father, Max, when he was 15 years old

The Tanenbaum family (Back row, left to right: Max, Faye, Esther and Simon Gottlieb, Joseph, Sam Katz. Middle row, left to right: Anne, Harold, Zaidy Abraham, Joey, Chippa Sura, Wayne, Sarah Katz. Front row, left to right: Minda Feldman, Marvin Katz, Frances Mandel)

Every Sabbath after lunch, I would sit with Zaida and *"vertatch a blatt gemarah"* – that is, study a portion of the Talmud. It was during these warm and meaningful discussions in Yiddish that I came to understand the importance for every individual never to forget from whence he came. He also taught me that you must never make money your god, that there is only *one* God, and that is the God in heaven.

Zaida was the one who told me that I must make business my *science*. He said, "Never get involved in a business you know nothing about." When I was still very young, I asked him, "Zaida, how did you become so wealthy?" His answer was, "My son, I would buy for a dollar and sell for two dollars, and make 1 per cent." I said, "But Zaida, that is not 1 per cent, that is 100 per cent." My grandfather looked at me with his beautiful, piercing blue eyes and said, "My son, I made it. It's 1 per cent."

I must tell you that I did not argue with my Zaida. I learned a basic lesson in business life. This is why I like to sell some of our assets from time to time and make Zaida's "famous" 1 per cent!

From my late father, Max, I learned a harder lesson, a lesson that would stand me in good stead in the years to come. For my dad, family came first and foremost. He was a man of vision and a man of strength. He was determined to make his children strong as well, to prepare them for the rough shoals in life. His philosophy was very simple but effective. In the words of Goethe's Faust, it was: "That which you inherit from your fathers, you must *earn* in order to possess."

It was those words that sustained me during the terrible economic upheaval that took place in this country in 1982, especially in the steel-fabricating business. With my dear wife, Toby, standing by my side, and with the love and support of our five children, we came through the crisis. And I was able to repay the bulk of our tremendous debt to the Canadian Imperial Bank of Commerce by April 26, 1989.

I would like to think that Zaida was watching me on that day. He would have understood why repaying the bank – our family's bank since 1924 – was one of the proudest days of my life. My Zaida knew, better than anyone, the importance of honouring a debt.

Both of my grandparents helped me to understand and take pride in what it means to be a Jew. By their words, and by their living example, they taught me to love and to honour our faith, our history, and the traditions of our people.

The Tanenbaum siblings, at 28 Glenwood Avenue, Toronto, 1947 (Standing, left to right: Harold, Joey. Sitting, left to right: Howard, Minda Feldman, Tauba Spiro, Larry)

One of my most precious memories dates back to 1935. On one particular Sabbath, my beloved grandparents had weekend guests: six rabbis with long beards. My late brother Harold and I nicknamed them "cowboys."

At lunch that day, I noticed that my grandmother was not eating. I left the table to ask her why she was not partaking of the Sabbath meal. She told me in Yiddish that there was not sufficient food. I immediately said, "Bubbie, it's not right that they should eat and you not eat." Her reply will always be with me, for she said, "*Yosseleben, gedenk ein sach mein kind, wie wenig a yid hat me muss zuteilen.*" – "My child, one must always share with one's fellow man, regardless of how little one has."

These words became the essence of my being.

Both Zaida's and Bubbie's commitment to Judaism was incredible. It permeated every aspect of their lives, and ours as children. Every Sabbath, we grandchildren would go to morning services at Maria Street Synagogue, and then to lunch at Bubbie and Zaida's home at number 138. All the preparations for the High Holidays would take place there, especially Rosh Hashana in the fall, and Passover in the spring.

My mom with her children, and Aunty Faye Tanenbaum and Aunty Sara Katz with their brood, all moved in with Bubbie and Zaida three to four days prior to the Holidays. Aunty Esther Gottlieb and her family lived just across the street. While the women helped Bubbie prepare the festive meals, we children had a great time staying out of their way. We would busy ourselves feeding the chickens that Bubbie kept in the backyard, or playing the well-known "Maria Street baseball" with the droppings from the horses.

Those were warm and happy days when we were young, and thinking of them can still bring me to tears.

Toby and Joey on their wedding day, May 22, 1955

In all our years together, my dear wife and I have been extraordinarily fortunate in so many, many ways. We have always felt *most* fortunate to be Canadians, especially growing up here during the Second World War.

This country gave all who came here — my grandparents from Poland, Toby's own parents from Russia — equality of opportunity unknown in Europe until the second half of this century. Canada gave us, as Jews, freedom unavailable almost anywhere outside of the State of Israel. Here in this incredible country, we have *always* had absolute freedom to practise our religion, and to pass on to our descendants the light of our faith and our historic heritage.

I believe this is a fundamental reason why Canada's 300,000 Jews are a presence on the national scene out of all proportion to our numbers. We have seized the infinite opportunities this country offers. Though we represent little more than 1 per cent of the total population, the contributions of Jewish Canadians to Canada's economic, scientific, and cultural development have been significant.

I, for one, believe that we have a special duty — to Judaism and to ourselves — to "earn what we possess," with generosity and with honour.

My Toby and I know what we owe to Canada and to our Jewish heritage. We only have to look at our five wonderful children. Our eldest son, Michael, has established his own, very successful, computer software company in Hawaii. Alan, our second boy, is with McDonald's here in Toronto. Our third

A recent photo

son, Marty, is a real-estate broker in Orillia, where his lovely wife Glenda Rosen has her own chiropractic clinic. Rob, our youngest boy, is a leading light in the hotel consulting business in Washington, D.C., working as a senior vice-president with the Host Marriot chain. And our one and only daughter, Susan, is president of our Loc-Pipe plant, the second-largest concrete and plastic pipe company in Ontario.

For us, our five children are the living proof of what it means to grow and to flourish in the most democratic and free nation on earth.

Looks like making bagels is serious business! The Bregman family in 1933 (Standing, left to right: my mother, Esther; Ruth; my father, Max. Sitting, left to right: Anne; Lou; Dora)

All Because of a Recipe for Bagels

The history of every country, someone once said, begins in the heart of a man or woman. Out of our hearts come memories and experiences, and we begin to weave the fabric that becomes a tapestry to be handed down to our children, and our children's children. When I look into my heart, and see the history of my family unfold, I know that I have been truly blessed with a legacy I am proud to pass on.

I've been asked to tell my story, to share the joys and sorrows that make up this intricate weave. Rich lives in poor times? Yes, we had that. My parents, Max and Esther Bregman, came to this country in 1919 from Erlich, Russia, newly married and eager to succeed. What a honeymoon — to come to Canada with nothing but a suitcase full of dreams, hearts full of hope and hands willing to work hard to prosper.

And work wasn't hard to find, not for Max Bregman. At nineteen he was already an experienced baker, learning the craft and mastering the art of bagel-making in Erlich. My dad got his first job on Spadina Road, at United Bakers, the only place in Toronto that made bagels. Who could have guessed that the simple bagel recipe he brought with him from Russia would become such an integral part of our lives and our success in Canada? That original formula

The stars of the Russian Bagel Bakery (left to right: Max Bregman, Alex Millman, Max Rabinowitz)

still survives today; if you live in Toronto, you've probably eaten a bagel based on the Max Bregman recipe at least once in your lifetime.

Work was hard and hours were long, but that didn't matter, as long as there was family and a place to call home. I can still remember the flat that was our first home – half of a rented house on Leonard Avenue, in the heart of Kensington Market. We considered ourselves rich with opportunity, love, and family. None of us had money – the bonds we shared were our dreams of success in Canada.

With the passion and faith of youth, my parents established roots. My mother was just seventeen when my oldest sister, Ruth, was born in 1921. Anne was born in 1924, and I came along in 1926. By the time my two younger sisters were born, Dora in 1934 and Edith in 1936, my mother was only thirty-two years old – a young woman by today's standards.

This was the Depression – perhaps not the best time to have a family of five children. But no matter. In 1936, after seventeen years of hard work and saving, my father opened his own business, the Russian Bagel Bakery, at 33 Kensington Avenue, with partners Alex Newman and Max Rabinovitch. In those days there was only one kind of bagel, and only one way to make it – the Max Bregman way. The bakery he bought came fully equipped with a horse and carriage, and cost $900 with a $10 down payment. A fortune in those days.

A new business meant a new home. The three families – the Bregmans, the Newmans, and the Rabinovitchs – moved in above the bakery. It's hard to believe that we were seventeen living in that small space: six adults, eleven kids, and only one bathroom, which we shared with the bakery employees. Twenty-three people using the same bathroom – and no one complained.

We didn't have much in the way of toys or playthings, but we did have "Jimmy," the bakery horse. He quickly became our family pet, and on Sundays my friends and I would ride him up and down the street.

The whole family participated in the business. It was a time when everyone got involved, from the smallest kids to the oldest adult. I was nine years old when I learned how to make bagels and the bakers taught me how to smoke. I felt like a man. While the men worked in the back, baking bagels, my sisters and mother cleaned, swept, and took care of the shop.

My first job was selling stringed mini bagels from a cart at Baldwin and Kensington, a dozen to a string, three dozen for a dime. It was wealth, especially when five cents could get you into the movies in those days.

My favourite day of the week was Thursday – pay day at the bakery. The bakers would get paid, and my mother would make a big dinner for the employees. The table would be groaning with the amount of food, and the beer would flow freely from a large keg sitting on the floor. After dinner my father would thank the employees for their hard work. In the early days, he would ask the bakers for a favour. You see, by Thursday there wouldn't be any flour left. If they wanted to work again the next day, they'd have to give back some of the money so he could buy more flour. Everyone did – no questions asked. It was understood that this was the only way everyone could survive. Everyone helped one another; no one went without.

I remember my Bar Mitzvah vividly. This was a simple, joyous occasion, the rite of passage that it was meant to be. The family gathered at Rabbi Aronoff's house, on Augusta Street, to celebrate. There were about thirty people there: family, the bakers, and some close family friends. The important thing was to be together – we all shared in the joys and sorrows of each other's lives.

*"One Way Only" Bregman
(my bagel-inspired nickname) comes of age*

The bakery was busy, but there were still reminders that the world was full of anger. During the war we had to change the name of our Russian Bagel Bakery to Canadian Bagel Bakery; the government wouldn't let us use the word "Russian." It was war – we didn't ask questions. We were just so fortunate to be in Canada at that time.

I went to Ryerson Public School, and then on to Central Tech, but I had to leave school – I was needed to help my father. The work was backbreaking, and all done by hand. It was nothing to lift a hundred pounds of flour at a time and throw it in the dough mixer. The mixed dough could weigh up to 750 pounds – quite a load to work with. I remember delivering bagels at 2 A.M. down darkened streets. My old friend Jimmy, the horse, was so well-trained that even when I nodded off at the reins he would stop at every customer.

By the time I was twenty, my dad decided to expand his horizons and opened Nu-Style Bakery on St. Clair Avenue, two blocks west of Dufferin – a full retail bakery that sold everything from bread to pastries to bagels. It was going to be a challenge getting a foothold in this mostly ethnic neighbourhood, but if anyone could do it, it was my father.

Business was dropping off. The war was over, but the good times hadn't begun. It made me restless. In 1947 I packed up and moved to California with visions of glamour, of Hollywood, of big cars and endless sunshine. I got a

Home again, and time to "get serious."
Lou and Yeta Bregman, 1952

lift with three veterans who were driving to California. I helped pay their expenses and got to see a piece of the country at the same time.

California was the land of milk, honey . . . and money! Within a month I was the head bakery man for a chain of restaurants called Simon's Cafeteria, making $330 a week. You can imagine a twenty-one-year-old loose in California with all that money to burn in his pocket. I wrote to my father and said, "Give up your business, pack up the family, there's gold here." Of course he didn't come. He had the bakery, and business was good.

From Simon's I went to work at Cantor's, a bakery/restaurant in Hollywood. The idea of a bakery counter combined with a full-service restaurant was something I'd never thought of before. I knew the concept was a winner, and years later it came to life at the Bagel King, on Eglinton Avenue West.

I stayed in California for three years, until 1950, when I was called home because my father's bakery had a fire. For a year I helped the family re-establish the business on St. Clair, but wanderlust was stronger than me, and in 1951 I left for Miami, Florida. My bagel-making skills came in handy, and soon I was employed at a bagel bakery. It was while I was there that I first had the opportunity to start my own business. A gentleman from New York wanted to go into the bagel business in Miami. Everything was set – we leased a place and stocked it with equipment.

Three days before we were set to open, the landlord insisted that we make his son a partner. That, I wasn't prepared to do. We couldn't work out a deal, and we walked away from it. My first big venture, and it never opened.

So what do you do when your bagel business falls apart? You go into landscaping, of course. I was young, I had a friend who was willing to be my partner, and the clincher was that my landlady's husband walked out on her, leaving the family business, a nursery, high and dry. As long as I paid the bills, I could have the nursery. And for all my lack of experience, we did all right. In fact, parts of the famous Parrot Jungle and the Saxony Hotel were our handiwork. I really loved what I was doing.

But now it was time to go home. I had sown my wild oats. Timing is everything, and obviously the timing was right, because very shortly after I arrived back in Toronto, I met my true love and wife-to-be, Yetta Perlman. We were married the next year, 1952.

It was then that I finally settled down and involved myself in business. I leased a place on Baldwin Street – Tasty Bagel Bakery – just down the road from where I sold those stringed bagels so many years before. I sold bagels wholesale to the other bakeries, but it was a struggle. Max Rabinovitch, my father's old partner and my competitor, approached me, and we eventually joined forces and became the Royal Tasty Bagel Bakery.

In 1957, I finally ventured out on my own, with the Bagel King, my dream of a retail bagel bakery come to life. We opened with a twelve-stool counter so that we could stay open on Sundays. Yetta was behind the counter, I was in the window making bagels. Who could have ever dreamed what would have happened on our first day of business? People came pouring in, everyone from women in fur coats to families with their kids, all wanting to try my bagels and standing six deep behind the stools, waiting to be served.

Right from the start, the Bagel King was a success. We expanded . . . and expanded . . . and expanded again to keep up with the demand. It wasn't long before the Bagel King was a Toronto institution, with three locations.

In 1964 I joined forces with Home Bread Bakery, a wholesale bread and roll bakery. Our biggest customer was the Hunt's and Women's bakeries, a five-hundred-store operation. When they threatened to find another supplier if we wouldn't give them a better price, I told my partner, "Either they buy us out, or we buy them out." We bought them out.

I've been very fortunate in my businesses, starting with the Bagel King in 1957, which quickly expanded to three locations, leading to the Pie Tree restaurant, and, in 1979, Bregman's Bakery Restaurant. Mmmuffins, Michel's Baguette, and now Second Cup . . . a cycle of family businesses that have developed into a legacy of success.

When I look back at this history, I can hear my father's voice. His motto was: Quality, always quality. Give the best and you can make a decent living. Never compromise on quality, on cleanliness. Make sure everything is perfect and don't sell anything that's less than that. These are words I have lived by.

I feel my true success has been where I have been truly blessed: with a loving wife; with my exceptional children, Michael, Jodi, Caurie, and Howard; and now my grandchildren, Jacob, Marci, Sarah, Allanah, Carrie, and Alex. Our family has always been rich, through good times and bad, with the love and support we have given each other.

A rapidly rising family count —
the Bregman family in 1996 (Back row,
left to right: son-in-law Leonard Glickman,
Marci Bregman, Jacob Bregman, Michael
Bregman, Lou Bregman, Howard Bregman.
Front row, left to right: Alex Glickman,
Allanah Glickman, Caurie Glickman,
Barbara Bregman, Carrie Bregman, Yetta
Bregman, Jodi Bregman, Sarah Bregman)

Pop and his boys! (left to right: Edgar Bronfman, Samuel Bronfman, Charles Bronfman)

Fifty Years Ago in Montreal

For those of you who were born after World War II and live in a world of Jewish emancipation, equality, and, yes, even power, what follows may be somewhat chilling.

I was born in 1931. Thus, at the outbreak of World War II, I was just beginning to understand the evil that was unfolding in Europe. Further, I had more than just passing information about the Canadian government's view of what, I much later discovered, was the Holocaust, because my father was then President of the Canadian Jewish Congress. I still recall, during those terrible years in the early 1940s, my dad and Saul Hayes going to Ottawa to meet with the prime minister and other influential ministers of the government and returning home with hopes that were high but belied the facts. Why were they going to Ottawa? To plead, beg, and exhort our government to accept the plight of European Jewry for the horror that it was, and to allow entry into Canada for those helpless people. *None Is Too Many*, by Irving Abella and Harold Troper, a book well worth reading, exposes the shocking position of our government in those years.

Why? How? Very simple. Canadian Jewry, like U.S. Jewry, like British Jewry and French Jewry, and indeed world Jewry, had no power. Further,

On vacation, Santa Monica, California, c. 1918 (front row, from left: Priscilla Berger Rosner and Samuel Charles Rosner, my maternal grandparents; Saidye Rosner, my mother)

157

anti-Semitism was as vibrant here as elsewhere (excluding, of course, Nazi Germany). Whether Canadian leadership was or was not overtly anti-Semitic, if one looked just under the skin, anti-Semitism was surely there.

Dad was a loyalist. He was so proud to be a Canadian, a member of the British Empire, that in speech after speech he urged Canadian Jewry to contribute in every way to the war effort. Our community's response was spectacular, in terms of volunteers to the Armed Forces and in every conceivable effort that could be made to help.

There was some form of recognition. My mother received the Order of the British Empire for her efforts in organizing the Jewish community of Montreal to support the Red Cross. But real recognition would have been a reversal of government policy regarding Jewish immigration to Canada. At the time, I didn't know, and no one spoke about Canada's refusal of Europe's beleaguered Jewry. Indeed Dad and Mother infused me with so much zeal for this country that at the tender age of seventeen I was quite ambivalent about the coming birth of the State of Israel. What would happen, I asked myself, if Canada and Israel ever went to war? Whose side would I be on?

Why do I write this? Because as we live in this age of Jewish renaissance, my thoughts go back more than fifty years to the way things really were. Just think about it. The days of the near annihilation of the Jewish people was not really so very long ago – a mere fifty years.

><

Gramps. I loved my gramps. He lived in Winnipeg and would come to Montreal every winter and take my cousins, Peter and Edward, and my brother, Edgar, and me for a sleigh ride on the mountain and then to Ben's Delicatessen for lunch. We would all eat too much, and Gramps would carry on an animated conversation with Ben (Kravitz) himself. In Yiddish, of course!

Gramps was indeed a gentle man – he was also my godfather, and I felt very very close to him. I was about sixteen when he asked me one day whether he should sell his threshing machine. (He had a farm outside of Winnipeg, which I had visited.) I asked him whether he was satisfied with the price, and he said yes. I asked him if he had need for the threshing machine, and he said no. I suggested that it seemed like a good thing to do, and he said that was fine and would I send the necessary telegram to say that he agreed to the proposition. Wow! Was I pumped up! My gramps had asked my advice about

In my grandparents' garden at 78 Ethelbert Street, Winnipeg (left to right: Phyllis Bronfman, Priscilla Berger Rosner, Samuel Charles Rosner, Minda Bronfman)

Samuel Charles Rosner on his threshing machine on the Rose farm, near Plum Coulee, Manitoba, c. 1920

a business matter! I was really somebody; not only was I worth consulting, I was given the additional responsibility of sending the telegram! Oh joy, oh joy!

It was many years later that the truth about all this came to me — and the truth is even warmer than the lovely story I have just recounted. It finally dawned on me that the real reason my gramps went through all this with me was because he could not write English. He had invented this whole ruse, asking my opinion and so on, in order to get me to write and send the telegram!

>-<

Another Gramps story. My mother and my aunt Freda used to exhort Gramps to drink his milk. He really didn't like milk, so he and I had an understanding: as soon as the women left the room, I would excuse myself to go to the washroom and pour most of the milk down the drain. Gramps did, however, like to drink something else. Seagram V.O. When asking for his evening cocktail, Gramps would always emphasize that he wanted a *big* drink, "with lots of V.O. in the glass, please." I remember asking him why a *big* drink. Surely, if he wanted more, it was available. "Oh, I couldn't do that," he would say. "Why?" I'd ask. "Well," he said, "my doctor told me I could only have one drink a day, but," he added, with a big twinkle, "he didn't say how much should be in that drink!"

>-<

One last Gramps story. He made my baldness look like a full head of hair! I would ask him whenever he came back from the barbershop whether they charged him half price. "Oh no," he would say, "they charge me double . . . Once to find it, and a second time to cut it!"

What a wonderful treasure of a human being.

The gang

Jakey Harris

My Grandfather, Jakey Harris

Milt Harris

All four of my grandparents came from the Pinsk region of White Russia and were in Canada by the early 1890s.

My paternal grandfather, his brothers (at least three), and his father and mother, came to London, Ontario, in 1886. Somehow, the whole family were always "Harris" in Canada, but had been "Yertzky" in the Old Country. Of course in Europe most Jews only began using last names since the eighteenth century and did not have a strong attachment to them. For many, therefore, it was easy to shed this vestige from the Old Country and shorten their names, or take on new Anglo-Saxon names as the Harrises did.

When they arrived in Canada, the Harrises immediately went into the junk business. My great-grandfather, Grampa, and his brothers were all partners in this enterprise. Although they had set up a junkyard in the centre of the city, Grampa also peddled throughout Southwestern Ontario with a horse and wagon. Standing four-foot-seven high, and wearing his ever-present bowler hat, Jakey Harris quickly became a well-known character in London.

But family battles over money were frequent and sometimes violent. By the First World War, only Grampa remained in London; his father and a brother had set up junk businesses in Detroit, and two other brothers did the same in Paris, Ontario. Then they also moved to Detroit. Eventually, the Harrises had also set up junk businesses in Ypsilanti, Michigan, and Toledo, Ohio. In London, Grampa went into partnership with his sons under the name J. Harris & Sons.

In those days, the junk business was almost exclusively Jewish. Our competitors in London were also Jews – the Leff family. Both William Leff and Jake Harris were married to strong-willed women. Neither Jennie Leff nor Dora Harris meekly followed their husbands' dictates. In 1921 the constant clash of iron wills between Dora and Jake became unbearable and they separated.

Not content to populate the junk business just with Harrises, my grand-father had, by 1913, brought over my grandmother's relatives, the Zalev family, and set them up in a small cottage across the street from the junkyard in London. By the end of the Great War, the Zalevs had gone into the junk business in Sarnia, Ontario, and in 1920 they moved to Windsor, where their descendants still operate one of the largest recycling companies in Canada. In the last sixty years, with the increasing sophistication of the business, as well as of succeeding generations of Jewish owners, the "junk business" became the "scrap business," which became the "secondary materials industry," and has now become the "recycling industry."

Although I had gone into the steel construction business in 1954 and had largely left the scrap business by 1957, and even after we had become a public company in 1967, I still retained the name J. Harris & Sons until the late 1970s. I always valued my connection with Jake.

Grampa was active in the small Jewish community. Although personally a non-believer, he even became president of his *shul*. But he spent a great deal of time in the non-Jewish community as well, particularly in politics. During a wild-drinking victory party for the mayor on the second floor of the city hall on election night, January 1, 1900, the floor collapsed. Grampa was listed in the obituaries next day in the *London Free Press*, but returned home from the hospital later that same day as full of life as ever. He was a lifelong dedicated Liberal. As he often told me, the proudest moment of his life was when he went to the 1905 Liberal Convention in Ottawa and shook Prime Minister Laurier's hand.

Nevertheless, London, like every other community in Canada and the United States, still exuded a strong aura of anti-Semitism. Jews were totally excluded from the real centres of power: the four private social and golf clubs, and most large financial and industrial companies. Some of the public restaurants refused to serve Jews, and at least one restaurant discouraged Jews until the mid-1950s. At a lower level, though, conspicuous Jews like Jake were accepted, somewhat as a badge of the "tolerance" of the community.

Amongst the children in the working-class neighbourhood, however, Grampa was revered. He loved kids, and any of them, including me, could come and "bum" a nickel or a dime from him. Many years later, after we had opened a steel branch in Windsor, a man saw our manager's truck parked at his house and inquired if the "J. Harris" on the truck was Jakey Harris from London. When he was informed it was, he told our Windsor manager how he had loved Grampa when he was a kid near the junkyard.

Once, when I was only five years old, I was sent over to Grampa's house, next to the scrapyard, to get him back to the small office for a phone call. Grampa was sleeping off his usual Saturday drinking bout. When I couldn't rouse him, I punched him as hard as I could in the eye. He sprang off the couch in a rage which immediately evaporated when he recognized his assailant. Grampa was quick to anger when sober, and often in a rage when drunk, but he never got mad at me.

Business was conducted very differently then. Empire Brass — now EMCO — was his largest account. They bought brass and copper scrap for remelting into ingots only from Grampa, their exclusive broker. Once a month, on a Friday afternoon, their offices were closed, and Jake would sit with their chief purchasers over several bottles of whiskey and agree on the following month's contract. Nothing was ever reduced to writing. His word was ironclad. He used to tell me, "If you can't believe a man's word, his signature isn't one bit better." Over the years, relying on other people's word got both of us into lots of trouble.

Like most other Jewish communities, no matter how small, London had two *shuls*. Both of them were Orthodox. In 1930, the two agreed to merge. My grandfather led about half of his congregation into the other *shul* but, when the rest refused to follow, one of the *shuls* sued the other. Grampa went to Toronto with a delegation from his group and hired the well-known Jewish lawyer Henry Rosenberg (father of Mr. Justice Alvin Rosenberg) and paid him a five-hundred-dollar retainer. The following year, however, before the case came to court, it was settled by a *Bet din* composed of rabbis from New York. The two

With Ethel Harris

shuls were to remain apart, but the fence separating their cemeteries was taken down. And so the merger was affirmed for the next world, but not for this one.

Six years later, in 1937, Henry Rosenberg, as chairman of the United Palestine Appeal, came to London to launch the year's campaign. Some of my grandfather's friends got him drunk — not an unusual condition for Grampa — and took him to the meeting. When Henry had finished speaking, my grandfather got up and said, "If Henry Rosenberg will give back the five hundred dollars he took from our community, I'll match it." Well, Henry sat down and wrote a cheque to the London campaign for five hundred dollars. But in 1937 Grampa didn't have that kind of money. Next day, he went around the community, but was only able to borrow $320, and he settled with the campaign for that amount. In 1972, thirty-five years later, I joined the Mount Sinai Hospital Board. Henry Rosenberg was its chairman. At the open house for new board members, Henry introduced me to his wife as "Jakey Harris's grandson."

The public battle over the *shul* merger left permanent enmities in the Jewish Community. Grampa never again spoke to anyone from his original *shul* who had refused to honour the merger agreement.

During the darkest days of the Second World War, in 1940, Grampa had a stroke that immobilized his enormous energy. Hardest of all, he had to give up drinking completely. But he would still become embroiled in raucous political arguments whenever I took him to the barbershop. Grampa listened to fifteen radio newscasts a day, and several times told me he intended to live until we won the war. On New Year's Day, 1946, my beloved Grampa went into a coma and died.

I will always be proud to be known as "Jakey Harris's grandson."

Mary Brody

—— ✢ ——

Mary Brody, My Mother

A photograph in a tortoiseshell frame sits on my desk — a beautiful sorrowing girl, a black ribbon of mourning in her hair. It is my mother, grieving for her own mother. Though she looks older, she was only a child of twelve.

The year was 1906. Mary Roth had just come to this country with her father when she learned that back home in Galicia, her mother, a strong woman of thirty-nine, had suddenly died. My mother would have to live with her uncle and aunt in a house crowded with children and overrun with cockroaches.

She soon found work in a garment factory and was paid a dollar a week, and in a few years Mary's two sisters immigrated, and finally two brothers, twelve and thirteen years old. Since my mother was the eldest, she felt responsible for the family, hoping that, although the girls had no chance for an education, the boys might attend school and have a better life. Instead, Morris and Ben drifted onto the streets, hawking newspapers and racing forums and hanging around pool halls.

My mother was only nineteen when she sued her father to force him to pay child support. She won her case. The judge ordered Joseph Roth to pay five dollars a week to the two boys, but my uncle Ben told me that my grandfather only paid for one week and the boys remained on the streets. Eventually they became bookies and wore immaculate pin-striped suits and drove huge

Ethel Harris

white Cadillacs. As a friend of mine who had worshipped Ben in his child-hood remembered, "He never had any dust on his shoes!"

The youngest brother, my uncle Moishe, remained in Europe, caught in the turmoil of the Great War. Homeless, he wandered from village to village, eating grass to stay alive. After the war my grandfather made no inquiries about his son, but in 1921 my father gave a friend travelling back to Prohata some money for Moishe's passage, and he was finally brought to Toronto. A sense of homelessness clung to Moishe all his life. When he trudged the sidewalks he looked down at the ground as though searching for roots, and he always wore a battered fedora perched on his head with the brim pulled down over his brow.

In 1918 my mother married Joseph Brody, one of the four founders of the Toronto Poale Zion, the democratic socialist wing of the Zionist movement. This was the party of Ben-Gurion, the Histadrut and the *kibbutzim*, the driving force behind the foundation of the State of Israel. Later my father became a leader in its offshoot, the Jewish National Worker's Alliance, and my mother became one of the founding members of Pioneer Women, now known as Na'amat. She was a committed member all her life. Long before the national-ism engendered by the establishment of the state in 1948, dedication to Israel was part of our way of life, bred into my very bones.

My parents' first child, a boy, born in 1922, was injured at birth and severely retarded. A daughter, born two years later, died of pneumonia at three months. During my mother's pregnancy with me, my parents did much soul-searching and finally decided to send my brother to the Ontario Hospital in Orillia so they could give me a normal home life. It was a wrenching choice.

When I was born, my mother, never having had the opportunity for an education, and loving knowledge for its own sake, dreamed of infinite scholastic achievement for me. After learning to read English on her own, and determined to raise healthy children, she studied books on nutrition. Back in the thirties, long before today's health-food craze, we ate whole-grain breads and cereals, wheat germ, the freshest fruit and vegetables, and actually took multi-vitamins.

My mother even studied psychology books about raising children. A woman who used to be my baby-sitter told me many years later that she once met my mother wheeling me in a stroller piled high with library books.

"Mrs. Brody, what are you doing with all these books?" she asked.

"They're for rearing my daughter. I read them very carefully," my mother laughed, "but I spank her anyway."

When it was time for me to go to school, my mother took me on the first day to show me how to cross busy Dundas Street. After that I was on my own.

I attended Givens Street Public School, an institution known for its tough kids. Many of them ended up in reform school, some for murder. On the way to school each day, a group of children taunted me with my Jewishness and beat me up. I never did find out how they learned I was Jewish. I was blonde and blue-eyed.

At the end of the first week I broke down and told my mother. She said nothing, but in a few days the attacks stopped; she had discovered that the children attended St. David's Separate School and had protested to their principal.

Aware as she was of anti-Semitism, and having the courage to fight it whenever possible, Mary Brody was not the usual ghetto Jew. She befriended the farmers in the country and invited several of my public-school teachers to our Seder. Never in our house did I hear the common Yiddish expression *"goyisher kop."* A person was a person, good or bad, whether he was Jewish or not.

Though most Jews were drawn to urban life, my mother longed for the country, especially in summer. All winter she looked forward to those few short months in various villages north of Toronto. At first Orillia, to be near her son, then Midland, Wasaga Beach, and finally many summers spent at Killarney Beach, where we bought a cottage of our own. There, many of her conflicts and ambitions abated. She was lulled into a kind of peace, a connection with nature. For me, too, those summer walks and swims were magical. That patch of blue lake we could see as we descended the hill from Lefroy was like a banner promising us a land of sun and calm days.

At the cottage we lived primitively, drawing water from a well, burning coal-oil lamps for light, and cooking on wood stoves. Of course there was no indoor plumbing. The most delicious food I've ever eaten were the berries, corn, and peas we often picked ourselves.

My mother had great plans for me: she wanted me to be a scholar, to cram into my head all the knowledge of which she had been deprived. And so, in her usual contending manner, she opposed my early marriage. Yet later she became reconciled to my life as a wife and mother. Even illness couldn't stop my mother's energies. Her losses, her hungers, her frustrations, all contributed to a hypertension she refused to acknowledge. Finally, at the age of sixty, after moving into a new cottage at Jackson's Point, where she could bask in her beloved countryside, she suffered a coronary and died.

PART FOUR

THE HOLOCAUST

Zaida, you face the camera as you face life, with the steadfast assumption that God will provide and God will protect

>‹‹

The Precious Box

I come from a family of artists. Only recently did I discover I was not alone in my inclination to draw and paint but part of an inherited connection. It was in 1983, when, quite by accident, I first met my aunt Marmish, my uncle Chaskell, and all the other Birnbaums.

Well, the truth is, I didn't really meet them in person, because sadly they died a cruel death in Treblinka, and on a date I don't even know and therefore cannot observe or remember with even a candle or a prayer. I met the Birnbaum family while on a grim mission – that eerie sorting-through of one's parents' belongings just after they have died and everything is still unchanged, as if they have only stepped out for lunch. My parents knew they could count on me to save the important things from falling into the hands of strangers – an embroidered tablecloth from Ozorow, a calendar showing my father as vice-president of the Ozrower Mutual Benefit Society, the trunk that travelled from Poland on the *S.S. Pulaski*, and, in the top drawer of a dresser, a worn paper box labelled Weldrest Hosiery, silk, size 9 ½. Inside the box were perhaps sixty yellowed pages of artistic Yiddish script, in ink once black but now grey. They were letters from Poland, the legacy of my mother's brother, her three sisters, and her parents. These letters had come to my mother, Idessa, from June 1930

Idessa's passport, July 18, 1930

Idessa Birnbaum (far right) with friends in an amateur theatre group in Ozorow, 1929

I feel an uncanny flash of recognition, as I had drawn this artwork myself

until our New Year's card posted on September 11, 1939, was returned, stamped "MAIL SUSPENDED, examined by censor 37."

In their correspondence, the Birnbaums paint a vivid picture of simple pleasures and very hard work, often related to art, my own field. Their work and my work might have been done by the same hand. I feel that uncanny flash of recognition when I look at the carefully drawn "O" of a decorated birthday card or the sparkle of the eyes in a pencil portrait. My hand responds as if I had done this artwork myself. My Zaida, my grandfather Yechil, used his handcrafting skills ingeniously. He had to, for in Ozorow one needed to be very cunning to earn a living other than by making shoes, making suits, or making harnesses. If Zaida were here now, I know what I would ask him:

Zaida, you stare so confidently at me as you face the camera, the same as you face life, in the absolute certainty that God will protect and God will provide. You say in your letters, "I know that the Creator is good, who runs the whole world only for the good." Zaida, I see you are always faithfully dressed in the shtramel (fur-trimmed hat), white stockings, and frock coat of the Chasid — and Zaida, how do you find time between Talmud and prayers to work at so many jobs and manage to set aside a good nadan (dowry) for Marmish and Raisel? You rush home from shul to your office, where you lend out money, mend holes in the szlotes (paper money), bake matzos for sale, carve the letters into a fresh tombstone (they say the cemetery dates back to the Spanish Inquisition).

Zaida, although you've been dead for fifty years, I see your concerns for your children are much like mine when you write:

Ozarów dn. 13/XI-1938r.   ʾʾ

[Ozorow Sun. 13/XI 1938 Portion of the Torah is Chaya Sara]

Dear daughter Idessa:

Now can you believe it, Marmish still doesn't want to get married. She says she's in no hurry. If only, God willing, it could be arranged for a matchmaker for daughter Raisel. I'll have to be patient until God sends along a match for her. Everything in its own time, it all depends on Him. We can do nothing until Providence decides the moment for a good match. And now to tell you that your letter dated *Portion Noah* we received *erev Shabbos Kodesh* [Holy Sabbath from the Portion Vayara] and also that you had a nice *esrog* [etrog]. And now we'll discuss that which you write about people thinking me wealthy. The truth is I have to borrow money from people, and then I get the reputation of being rich. And in the Talmud it states: "One who is not lame, not blind, and not crippled and he behaves as if he is, does not die of old age until he has one of these afflictions," a self-fulfilling prophecy. This is a bad habit. If I am accused of being a rich man, then I won't die until I am a rich man. May God grant us all good things that we should be able to raise our children with *naches* [joy] and comfort . . .

Your father, Yechil Birnbaum

Zaida, if you were more of a heretic and less of a believer we might have had this conversation face to face, but I do envy you your faith and respect your knowledge of the Talmud. Curiously, Zaida, I notice you sign all your letters Yechil Birnbaum except that very last letter of August 24, 1939, exactly one week before Hitler invaded Poland. Why in that letter only did you include your middle name, Yechil Yitzhak Birnbaum?

My Bubba, my grandmother Yochwid, adds a postscript to Zaida's letter:

> . . . I had a dress made for myself and I bought a pair of black patent leather shoes for the holidays. I know this will make you happy. But I still haven't bought myself a *sheitel* [wig]. I don't know which kind to get, a straight one, or one with curls. I send you warmest regards my dear children.
>
> Your mother, Yochwid Birnbaum

The Birnbaums outside their house in Ozorow, 1938 (left to right: Marmish, Yechil, Yochwid, Raisel, Chaskell)

More letters in the box, from Sarah, Marmish, Raisel, Chaskell (their brother), even Bubba. Shtetl life as revealed through these letters is an absurd mix of the cultivated and the plebian. Imagine books, theatre, and fine clothes in houses with no water or electricity;[*] black silk frock coats, fur-trimmed dresses, and patent leather shoes but no toilet; evening meetings of the Zionist club, chess club, and acting groups by kerosene lantern; hand-embroidered linens on beds that were simply straw, the laundry done every two months when a hired girl would boil the clothes; fancy braided challahs glazed with egg whites and sesame seeds, crispy brown potatoniks, but no oven — you carried these to the bakery early Friday, when the oven would still be warm from the morning breads.

* Electricity came in 1932 to a few houses.

The letters written in the early 1930s speak of a quiet, idyllic life for young people, since there was little or no work. By the end of the decade, it had all changed. Marmish, my mother's sister, writes:

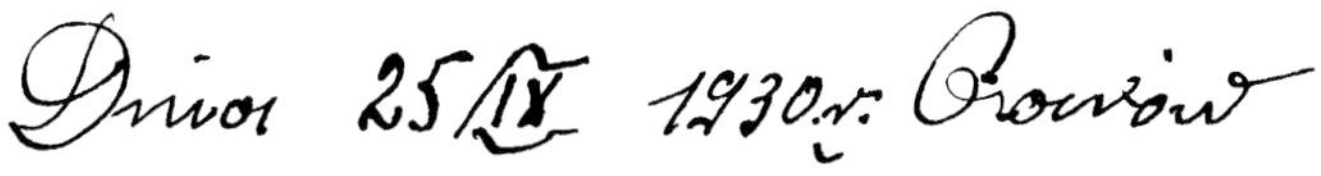

Dniat 25/IX 1930.r. Osorow

[25/IX 1930 Osorow]

Dearest sister Idessa:

. . . Things are very cosy here in Ozorow. The young people are having a good time, we dance all night long, we leave for the dance at ten o'clock and we return at six in the morning. And today there's a play at the theatre called *Always a Fool*. I'm thinking of going. . . . I'm making a living and sleeping in my socks. . . .

6/XI 1933 Ozorow

. . . Today we made lemon jam. It came out very well, and when we have a chance we'll send you some. . . . I'm sending you a needle; it's been lying around since before Rosh Hashana and I kept forgetting to send it. . . . Let me know how many corners you want the table napkins to have. Do you want all four corners embroidered or just one? . . .

We often go to the community hall; and even better, they rented a separate place near the cultural club where the Rabbi was once beaten up. . . .

6/X 1936

. . . I didn't have time to write because we were busy sewing blouses and white trimmed dresses. . . . You ought to know that I would really like to go to Canada, but I won't tell my father because, as you know very well, he's against my going. He doesn't approve of the people who are emigrating. As for me, I am bored and indifferent. . . . Write and tell me how much it would cost to bring me over. Maybe I would go. . . .

24/I 1939

. . . They're driving all the Jews out of Poland and taking everything away as they did in Germany, and since my dowry is still intact, I have six hundred dollars. So dear sister, if you have any pity at all and don't want to see the death of me, my plan is to quickly get married here in Poland,* and you should make an application to bring us both over. . . .

24/VIII 1939

[the last letter, the war began one week later]

. . . Chaskell is in the biggest hurry to leave, since he reads the Polish newspaper every single day. If he had wings he would fly to America. Idessa, we are getting black with worry. . . .

Dear Aunt Marmish, I reply. I wish you had found the wings to fly to America. The woods here have fine tall trees like those you once described in Ozorow. Here you would have been free to work as an artist. You could have designed book jackets, theatre sets, wallpapers, car-pets, fabrics. Here, your children could have joined the public library, taken the subway to a downtown concert, or to the museum or planetarium.

We sleep in separate beds in separate rooms, while your whole family slept in two beds in the same room. We have too many of the world's goods and comforts, and you had too few. But the quality of life, here, is really not much better than it was when you were growing up in Ozorow. Then, parents were always close by, and food was farm fresh and home baked, not refrigerated. You had swimming and skating on the pond in the woods, books from the local store, and plenty of music and dancing and acting. There was poetry and artistry in the festivals of Purim, Chanukah, Succoth, and Shevuot.

Marmish, I am looking at the wonderful Parochet you sent us to raise funds for your emigration. The two lions of Judah are so jolly and inventive, they make my heart sing. Did you choose that particular shade of sunflower-yellow embroidery thread so it would look like gold? This Parochet is truly a great work of art. Marmish, it has verve. It is too precious to keep at home, so we gave it to the museum.

For the same postage we usually heard from everybody. My uncle Chaskell writes:

---

* Marmish married Yosel Hirshorn in late 1939. Yosel did not survive.

Left: Marmish and Raisel designed and worked this Parochet and sent it to Canada to raise funds for their hoped-for emigration (silk embroidery on linen, 3'6" x 4'6")
Right: During Shevuot, the raiselach glowing in the windows of the Birnbaum house were admired by the whole town

Ozorów dn. 19/V 1938 r.

[Ozorow 19/V 1938]

Dear sister,

. . . The matzos came out fine and we made some money. It was a happy Passover, with lots of wine and lots of visitors. Now it's time for me to pass before the "Wajskava Commission" on June 18. I'd still like to see your home and our brother Shlomo. I haven't lost hope: the future for the young Jewish people in Poland looks far from good.

. . . I read in the paper that farmers from Poland could get into Canada for 1,000 dollars. I don't know if you have to show them the money to buy the land. If you see anything in the Canadian paper about any of this, let me know in your next letter. I see . . . when your husband is away at work you enjoy being with your smart and pretty daughter Rifke [Rosalie]. . . .

Chaskell, you are the one I miss the most.
Just 18 you were in 1939.

Ozorow 14/VI 1939

. . . There was a by-law passed that every shop had to have a signboard and all the signs had to be the same colour; I know this kind of work very well so I made a little bundle. . . .

Dear Uncle Chaskell, you are the one I miss the most. Just eighteen you were in 1939, the youngest of the family, yet the wisest. How I wish we had all been as wise as you, including the Canadian government, which closed its doors on so many Jews.[*]

I miss sharing our interests in lettering, reading, and language. My son Jordy recently carved a sign into a solid piece of pine as you mention you made to designate Jewish shops, which Poles were forbidden to enter. Together we might have started a sign-painting business, or sat for each other's portraits in shaded HB *pencil.*

Chaskell, I'm looking at your two pencil sketches of Idessa and Shlomo, your sister and brother, done in Ozorow from photographs and sent to Canada. I compare them with the photos, and I approve of your artistic licence. The eyes have a liveliness that reaches from your hand to our hearts. I remember one time Zaida mentioned you were too busy sketching to add a postscript to his letter.

And the last letter, a week before the war:

Ozorow 14/VIII 1939

. . . I'm having a very good time these days. Every day I go to the woods, where I make new friends and we all take photographs of each other. I had a picture taken of me like the one I'm sending you [it has been lost]: you'll notice that you now have a big brother, much different from the one you left behind. . . .

. . . I send warm regards to your husband and child.

Your brother, Chaskell

This New Year's card from Canada, sent on September 11, 1939, was returned, stamped "mail suspended."

None Is Too Many, by Irving Abella and Harold Troper, documents the anti-Semitic immigration policies of Canada. Between 1933 and 1945, during Mackenzie King's third term as prime minister, only 5,000 Jews were admitted.

Rosalie Wise Sharp (extreme right), 1943, age 8

I put away the precious box of letters for now, but I visit the Birnbaums again from time to time — Yechil, Yochwid, Sarah, Marmish, Raisel, and Chaskell — my family, a company of artists, decent folk. Maybe we would have been great friends — maybe not. But we would have enjoyed each other and *shepped naches* (realized joy) from our children's achievements, some of which would likely have been greater than ours. I'll say goodbye, then, for now.

With Fräulein

>‹‹

From There to Here

Most of those who have contributed to this anthology are second generation Canadians, writing about happy memories and recounting nostalgic anecdotes, as well as the difficulties of growing up Jewish in a young, gentile country. Most lived through the terrible Depression of the 1930s and went on to experience a more prosperous and hopeful era in the 1940s.

My life is the other side of the coin. The thirties were the good years; the forties were the hard ones. I was born into the Europe of Adolf Hitler.

I was an only child and never knew the kind of *Yiddishkeit* that I later encountered in Canada. My parents and grandparents were secular Hungarian Jews. I heard no Jewish expressions, nor did I even know anybody who kept kosher. My grandfather worked as a public-sector veterinarian who oversaw large tracts of land in the countryside. My mother was his third child, born in 1911. After World War I there was a backlash against the Jews of Hungary following a failed uprising whose leaders included many Jewish students. Colleagues who wished to protect my grandfather asked him to convert so they could help him keep his position. He absolutely refused, and instead took early retirement from the civil service — even though he had served as an army officer during

My maternal grandfather, Ignac Szabo

My Father, Max Manoville, age 38

My mother, Elisabeth, and father in Italy, 1937

the war. He was forced to take a lesser job in the private sector, a chain of events that took a toll on the family and made a strong impression on my mother.

On the other side of my family tree, my paternal grandfather deserted his wife, leaving my father's mother to raise her three children alone. My father became the man of the house at a very young age and managed to prosper in business very quickly. He married off his two younger sisters, providing a dowry for each, as was the custom. He also built a fine house for his mother, with beautiful gardens that I can still remember clearly. As a confirmed bachelor, my father soon began collecting paintings, fine rugs, and furniture. He met my mother when he was thirty-eight and she was twenty-two, and they married within months. My parents thought of themselves as good Jews, which meant making charitable donations and observing the High Holidays.

By the time I was born, Hitler had been in power for three years. Our first shock came when my mother's brother was suddenly forced to return to Hungary from Vienna, where he had been living. His arrival forced the family to consider emigrating, but everything seemed so peaceful at that stage that these thoughts just faded away. I, of course, knew nothing of the larger political situation, living a carefully planned routine under the care of a German governess whom I called Fräulein. This highly qualified gentile woman was hired to teach me German, but as a response to the times, my father would not allow it. My governess and I led a totally separate life from my parents. Fräulein had complete control over my serene yet disciplined childhood, and I loved her dearly. In the summer we would go to our house in the country with my mother's parents and our cook, receiving only occasional visits from my parents, who vacationed in Italy. Looking back, I now see the sad irony that, had the war not intervened, I may never have become as close to my parents as I later did. Still, those summers in the country were enchanted times for me. To this day, when I am upset or in pain, I merely conjure in my mind those sun-speckled woods, the smell of the crisp air, and the total quiet that surrounded me.

And yet, storm clouds were gathering across Europe. Jews were slowly denied access to universities and other venues of community life. My parents thought the best way to shield me from anti-Semitism was to send me to a Jewish elementary school. I felt alien and stupid at first, knowing so little about Judaism. But this feeling was quickly displaced by my excitement at learning how to read, a priceless gift that allowed me to lose myself in books to escape the fear and confusion of the days to come.

It was not Fräulein but Joska, my father's devoted manservant, who accompanied me to school. Young thugs waited near the school, jeering at us, sometimes beating up the children. I turned to Joska, whom I considered my friend, and asked him what caused this hate. What did we do? For the first time, he could not answer me. "Don't pay any attention," he said. "It is only because you are Jewish." I also remember noticing caricatures of Jews in newspapers. The men were cruelly ugly. How could my blond, blue-eyed father be like that? It was true, he did smoke cigars as portrayed, but that was all. I started looking speculatively at my beautiful mother and myself in the mirror. A nagging feeling began to grow: there must indeed be something wrong with us. I ached to be the same as everybody else. Then I heard the adults talk of the Nuremberg laws and gossip about who converted and who did not. I may not have understood all the details, but the meaning sunk in.

During the war, my mother's newly widowed sister came to stay with us from her home in a part of Romania that had been Hungary before World War 1. She was so homesick that she left us to go back, and soon became the first — but not the only — victim in our family. That marked the first time I heard the term "deportation." My forty-three-year-old aunt was taken to Auschwitz and never came out again. My mother and her family never forgave themselves for letting her go back to her home town.

In March 1944, the German army occupied Hungary and installed the Arrow Cross, the Hungarian Nazi party, to govern. A polite, good looking German officer moved into our home. He clicked his heels, kissed my mother's hand, and confided to us how much he loved music. But that did not stop my terrified mother from visiting an old childhood friend who held a high position at City Hall. When she begged him to tell her whether we should flee, the man broke out in a sweat and practically stuttered as he tried to reassure her that we were perfectly safe. In any case, it was too late to get out.

Already, Jews could not own businesses or employ staff. At night, as I lay in bed, I heard a lot of commotion as valuables disappeared from our house — pictures, carpets, jewellery. My parents began to doubt friends and employees of long standing. Some joined the Nazi party. Even Joska grew a Hitler moustache to play along, and my father never forgave him for that. Still, after the war, Joska did return all the valuables my father had entrusted to him when we were forced to give up our home. It turned out the polite German officer was in charge of setting up a ghetto, and we had to move in with friends

Me, age 4

At a birthday party, 1940. I am in the centre, with my cousin Peter Szabo on my right and my cousin Leslie Benisz seated on the floor to my left. Of the group pictured here, we three were the only ones to survive the Holocaust.

in a smaller apartment. When we were forced to wear the yellow star, my mother was so overwhelmed that she refused to go out in public. So I began to do the shopping, setting out on my bike through the ghetto. My mother had also never cooked, cleaned, or done laundry – she did not know how. My father and I tried to help. It was as if our roles had suddenly been reversed; now I had to protect my mother. I never stopped protecting her until she died years later in Canada.

We moved to smaller and smaller rooms in the ghetto. I remember the day my mother broke down sobbing, saying she had had a premonition that we were all about to perish. She was desperate to see her parents. She said she wanted to die with them. To calm her, my father decided we would visit my grandparents in nearby Pest for a few days. I remember holding my parents' hands as we walked out of the ghetto, carrying nothing, so as not to arouse suspicions. We tore off our yellow stars and got onto a streetcar without anybody noticing us. My grandparents were also running a risk, since guests were not permitted. A Jewish doctor, who was allowed to come and go from the ghetto, stopped by that day and the next. But on the third day there was no sign of him. We sensed something was very wrong. My father was anxious to go back to check on his sisters, whom we had left behind in the ghetto. Fortunately, the others stopped him. A day later we found out the ghetto had been closed.

During the previous weeks, my father had stood in line for hours at the Swedish legation in order to get *schutz* (protection) passes for us from the diplomat Raoul Wallenberg. Now, armed with those papers, my father went to see the infamous Adolf Eichmann, who was in charge of the "Final Solution" to the so-called "Jewish problem" and was in Hungary just then. Eichmann accepted my father's offer: he would spare sixteen people from the Jewish ghetto in exchange for my father's business, a warehouse filled with leather hides that had a value at the time of U.S. $80,000. The deal was done. But the horror was yet to come; nobody from the ghetto could be found. All had been herded into a brick factory then loaded onto cattle cars. It is impossible to describe the depth of my father's despair. He felt he had deserted his sisters, even though there was nothing he could have done had we been there.

How bizarre! While Eichmann is looking after the "Final Solution," he gives my father a note for this large sum of money. And as the note survived, it caused debates between my parents here in Canada, where we arrived poor. Father could not bring himself to turn it in to the German government for damages. He felt any payment would have erased the death of his sisters and friends.

While we were living with my grandparents, my father went out on an errand and failed to return. Days passed, and we heard nothing from him. By now the radio blared out the German victories, the "Horst Wessel" anthem, and the never-ending stream of new rules for Jews. My uncle arranged to get my grandparents, my mother, and I into the Convent of the Sacred Hearts, which already had many Jewish children masquerading as Catholics in its boarding school. The adults hiding there included the chief rabbi of Pest. The nuns who took us in were brave and sincerely wanted to help, although, as I learned much later, they received neither support nor encouragement from the Vatican. While at the convent I went to mass every day, strangely comforted by the Latin chanting and smell of incense. Together with the calming presence of the nuns, it felt like a safe haven.

After three weeks we were thrilled when my father suddenly reappeared — fifty pounds lighter than when he left. Uniformed officers had stopped him on the street and sent him with a group of men to walk toward the German border. His Swedish passport meant nothing; they simply tore it up. It was Wallenberg who located the men and brought them back to Budapest. Although his collar was inches too big, my father was in a buoyant mood. Under his arm he had a small espresso maker and a pack of cards. We were together again.

We had made it to the late fall of 1944. Those who listened to the BBC knew that the war was all but over. Still, the German occupiers and their associates in the Hungarian Nazi party continued to murder Jews with zeal, as if they

The family, in 1944 (left to right: Father, me, Mother, my cousin Livia, and Livia's mother, my aunt Manci Szabo)

1944

had all the time in the world. There had been raids at the convent, although nobody had yet been discovered. One woman decided to risk leaving for the countryside with her child, and she gave my mother and me their identification papers, saying she could get new ones from her parents. It was a precious gift. We studied our new names and identities literally day and night. I was letter perfect in all the details of my new brothers, grandparents, and so on, but still my mother was so agitated she would wake me in the night to quiz me.

As the danger increased, the nuns finally evacuated the convent. I watched from the windows as the children lined up on the street, shivering in the cold until they were transferred – I know not to where. Forty years later I met one of those girls, and she told me she was hidden by a relative and that she eventually converted. Her grandson does not even know the family was Jewish. Our family made its way in shifts to a Swedish safe house. I was aware of the danger, but still did not realize that those who were taken away were most likely dead or suffering beyond belief. It was my job to act unperturbed, so as not to add to my mother's worries. At that very young age, I learned not to show my emotions.

When our building was hit by a bomb, we moved into the unheated basement, where we stayed with no beds or blankets, surviving on thin soups doled out by the Swedes. In these final days of the war, the Nazis and German soldiers were still committing atrocities, sometimes shooting groups of Jews on the banks of the Danube.

By the time we were liberated by the Russians, I had lice, dysentery, and could barely walk due to severe frostbite. My parents sat me in an old pushcart they found and trudged toward our home. Our house was occupied by soldiers, but we found a room, left by Joska, at my aunt's place. Besides my aunt's bedroom set and spotless linens, there was a shelf full of ripe quince – a heavenly smell.

Now, in the spring of 1945, word got around that we were alive, and so former friends and neighbours returning from labour and concentration camps came to stay over with us, recounting their stories of horror, each one in fact a miracle of survival. When I returned to school that fall, I realized that none of my friends had survived; children of my age did not come back from Auschwitz. Parents who had lost children cried when they saw me. Walking past empty houses where I had previously played was almost unbearable. I found out that my best friend, whose father was a pharmacist, never did go to

*Ujpest, 1945. The only Jew in the class.
(I am in the front row, 2nd from left)*

the brick factory the day the ghetto was liquidated. The druggist gave his child poison, then his wife, and then himself.

In 1946 we moved to Pest, and in 1948 to Vienna. I later heard that our whole town was torn down. The twisting streets were replaced by a new suburb – even the cemetery was moved. My childhood vanished during the war, and my past seems to have been wiped off the earth. The only reminders are my father's papers, which sit in my filing cabinet, some handwritten documents with antiquated stamps on them from between the two world wars. We came to Canada in 1952, a time when neither the government nor Jewish institutions helped newcomers in the way they do now. Although my mother spoke English, she had trouble adjusting and died of cancer at age fifty-two, just eleven years after her arrival. My father, sixteen years her senior, never complained and lived until he was ninety-one. Having survived the Holocaust, nothing ever seemed too difficult.

For me, the kind of Jewishness that binds families and weaves happy memories was created not by my elders, but by my children. Today, I am the one who cooks Friday night dinner for my grandchildren – toddlers to teenagers. They will be the ones to tell sweet nostalgic anecdotes of their childhood. And that is as it should be.

Jeanette and Julia Podolski at Swansea, near Cardiff, 1946

From Cardiff to Canada

In December of 1992, I was invited to go to Berlin for a UJA (Karen Hayesod) conference to address a group of European chairmen. For me it was a very emotional experience, unlike any other I have had. For the first five minutes, I spoke in German — a language I heard at home. This is how I began.

"Were it not for Hitler, I would have been able to say to you tonight '*Ich bin eine Berlinerin.*' I would have been able to tell you about the home my parents, Eli and Max Podolski, lived in on Passauer Strasse. I would have been able to tell you about my father's *heren bekleiderunk* [men's clothing] and *shoe varren gesheft* [shoe factory outlet] on Berliner Strasse, or about the synagogue they attended on the Sabbath and Yomtov on Fersahner Strasse, or even about Charlottenberg, where my grandparents lived. . . . "

During my three days in Berlin, I visited some of those places that I had heard about since my earliest childhood. Of course, my parents' home is no longer there. Even the street name has been changed, to Ethaler Strasse. What remains of the synagogue where my parents were married are two pillars in front of the Berliner Gemeinde Haus.

My parents belonged to that group of Jews who felt that Germany was a haven from Jewish persecution and poverty. They were modern, enlightened,

Jeanette and Julia with our grandmother Margaret Moses, Cardiff, 1944

191

First Zionist Purim poses, Cardiff, 1948

and yet orthodox in their observance of Jewish tradition. Life was very comfortable and serene. But all that changed with the rise of Hitler. Nevertheless, like most Jews, the perpetual optimists, they did not hasten to leave and stayed until almost too late.

It was the terror of Kristallnacht that finally brought the message home to them that things were really as bad as they appeared. When the next day the Gestapo called for my father, he miraculously managed to evade them and left for England on the first plane that was available, which happened to be on the Sabbath. Being uneasy about travelling on the Sabbath, my father asked the rabbi for advice and was told that in matters of life and death, life took precedence over the Sabbath. That advice proved to be very fortuitous, as the next plane out after the Sabbath crashed, with no survivors.

My parents were the lucky ones – lucky that they had relatives who could bring them over. The rest of our family were not that fortunate. And this is how a Jewish girl and her sister, Jeanette, were born in a coal-mining town called Cardiff, in the south of Wales.

This was a time when Jews from Europe found refuge in all sorts of places, and for my parents, who were "true Berliners," Cardiff was their salvation. The war years were not easy for them, but compared to what they left behind in Europe, it was paradise. However, it left its mark on them, so when the tensions of the cold war grew, they decided to emigrate to Canada, as far away as they could get from any impending conflict.

So in May 1948, at the age of four and a half, I, with my parents and sister, aged eight, sailed off to New York on the *S.S. America*, first class. Decades later, when my mother was sorting through old passenger lists, she discovered that on our deck was the Kennedy family. We were to make that journey across the ocean two more times. The decision to make a firm commitment in Canada seemed too daunting for my parents. It wasn't until the return trip back to England that we realised Canada was indeed the place to begin our new lives.

Obviously, our adjustment as new immigrants was not smooth. We first settled in Montreal, and my father set up a leather goods factory, where he manufactured ladies' purses. Unfortunately, business ventures with various partners turned sour, and the French language posed a problem for my parents even in those days. My father felt Ontario was the place to go, and so in 1954 he relocated his business in Toronto. At that point he also realised that my mother was the best and only trustworthy partner he could have.

The family on board the Queen Elizabeth *on our second voyage to Canada, 1949*

After a very unsettled childhood, I was finally beginning to feel that Toronto would be my permanent home. I grew up on the fringes of the established community, not quite fitting in to any particular social group. Even though my sister and I did not have a Jewish day school education (only some private tutoring and some *cheder* classes), we retained our strong Jewish identity because of our upbringing at home. One of my earliest memories, for example, is of seeing my father during his morning prayers. He always considered it *mazeldik* if I kissed the square tefillin which rested on his forehead.

The first synagogue we attended in Toronto was the Gilgorm, off Eglinton Avenue. Going out during the Yiskor service together with other young people was a social highlight. This was the opportunity for my sister and I to mingle and socialize with members of the *shul* and to make friends.

I recall vividly how, during the Israel Bonds Appeal on Kol Nidre, I marvelled that there were Jews who could buy tens of thousands of dollars' worth of bonds and dreamt that perhaps one day I could be one of those purchasers. It was my first introduction to communal fundraising.

I attended Northern Secondary School, on Mount Pleasant Avenue, where I was one of a handful of Jews. During my five years there, I was very much aware of my Jewishness. I had to learn how to decline going out with non-Jews, and I became very adept at explaining to our principal the significance of every Jewish holiday and why I could not attend school.

However, none of this hindered me from fully participating in all the school's extra-curricular activities, which I thoroughly enjoyed and which helped to shape me as a person. When it came time to sing Christmas carols,

Julia and Jeanette, Montreal, 1953

or Handel's *Messiah* at Massey Hall, I only mouthed the words – this was my personal compromise.

At the beginning, our social lives revolved around attending functions with our parents at the New World Club, a group of immigrants from similar backgrounds who enjoyed each other's company. My parents never hired baby-sitters for us, we just went along wherever my parents happened to go. It seemed the most natural thing to do in those days.

The first years in Toronto were difficult for our family, with major set-backs. Only one year after arriving from Montreal, my father was involved in a severe car accident and was hospitalized at Mount Sinai for twenty-one months. In the end, his right leg had to be amputated. We had no family, no medical connections, and found it impossible to find the proper medical consultations.

My mother had to attend to the business, bring up her two daughters, and also care for my father in the hospital, who would eat only her kosher food. We brought the food to him every day, travelling by two buses and the subway. I often wonder how we survived those first few years.

But thank G–d, some good always emerges from difficult and stressful times. A romance developed between by sister and the chief resident, Doctor Benjamin Massouda, and in time they were married.

My father lived for another thirty productive years. He worked full time, travelled, and enjoyed life to the fullest. He marched down the aisle

A cheerleader at Northern Secondary School, 1960

On my wedding day (left to right: Max and Eli Podolski, Julia, Henry, Golda and Israel and Koschitzky)

*The Dividends. Our grandchildren
(left to right) Marnina, Yadin, Nediva, Adir,
Adriel, Merav, Ariel. Our latest grandchild,
Yisrael, was born after this photo was taken.*

at the weddings of several grandchildren and experienced the birth of great-grandchildren.

At the age of eighteen, in my last year of high school, I was fortunate to meet my partner-to-be, Henry Koschitzky, son of Israel and Golda, and brother of Saul. Their family history, although vastly different from mine, still had the same thread running through it, as they also survived the war years in Russia and came to Canada as new immigrants in 1948. Henry and I both feel very fortunate that our families were among the lucky few who survived the Holocaust and were successful in rebuilding strong Jewish families in Canada. After thirty-four years of marriage, we can be proud of our four children – Sareena, Hartley, Jonathan, and Leelah – their spouses and our grandchildren.

When I reflect on our past, I come to the conclusion that our survival and what we possess today are not the result of any wise decisions, but rather a gift from G–d, and, having been blessed with this gift, that it is incumbent upon me to share in every way possible my good fortune with the rest of Klal Yisroel.

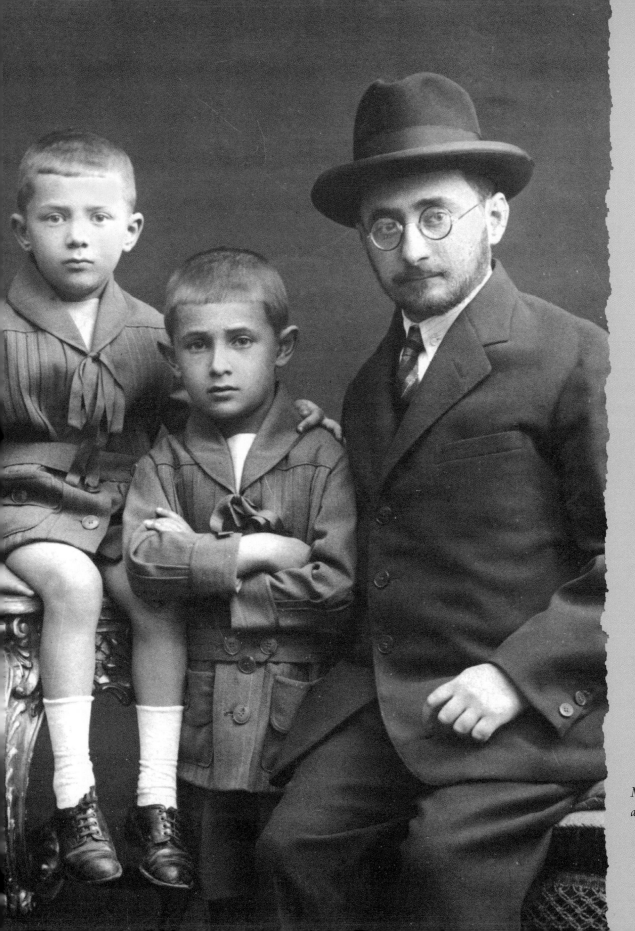

Me, my brother, Chaim,
and my father, Henoch

Danger and Daring

When one is confronted with danger, daring action is required. That was a lesson I learned repeatedly as I outran and evaded the Gestapo during the Second World War, sometimes just hours before their arrival. Risk-taking for me was a matter of survival.

During Pesach of 1937, an incident occurred at our Seder table that brought this notion home to me in a powerful way. Until then I hadn't understood that people could take daring risks to try to save themselves. We lived in the beautiful and ancient Polish city of Kraków, part of a large and historic Jewish community. My father was a middle-class merchant. Living with us at the time was a professor from Dresden, Germany. Because he was a Polish Jew with no German citizenship, he had been deported back to Poland. Taking care of its own, the local *kehilla* had assigned one of these refugees to every household, and that is how he came to be living under our roof.

The professor sat in respectful silence as my father conducted the Seder, but during the concluding prayers, he broke into tears. "Mr. Grossman!" he exclaimed in German. "Wake up! What happened to me will happen to you! You have a beautiful family, you're a well-to-do man. It is so easy for you to liquidate everything and get away from here! You must do it! I beg of you!"

My mother, Leah, c. 1917, at age 17

197

The family in Kraków, 1926 (left to right: Shanka, Leah, Gutka, Chaim, Alex, Henoch)

How well I remember my father carefully explaining in his imperfect German, for the better part of an hour, why such a course of action would be impossible. For one thing, he had two daughters who were approaching the age of marriage. Where would they find husbands if the family suddenly moved away? And should he just abandon the business and factory that took so many years to build up? What about all the goodwill and business connections he had established?

Tragically, like so many others, my father would not budge in his logic. The professor could not change his mind. After a while he moved on, and we never saw him again. But his words rang in my ears that night and on many future occasions. This man deeply influenced me, because I soon realized that he was absolutely right. We were on the brink of desperate times, and desperate measures were needed.

Even after the shocking brutality of Kristallnacht in November 1938, many people didn't want to believe that the evil within Germany would spread. Still a teenager, I had studied at a Jewish business school and worked for a friend of my father. I hoped to go to a college of business administration. Life was calm and pleasant in Kraków, and we thought it would always be that way.

Then, in September 1939, the Germans invaded.

For three days, things seemed quiet. The next morning I bid my mother goodbye as I left the house, certain I would return for lunch as usual. I did not come back.

Chaos reigned on the streets. People were panicking, shouting, "The Germans are coming! The Germans are coming!" Downtown, some friends of mine had a horse and wagon. "We are running away. Do you want to join us?" they asked. Up I went onto the wagon, and I never looked back.

Travelling east, we reached the occupied city of Zamosc. Some German officers, who were openly shooting civilians, turned their guns on us. A Jewish girl distracted them and we were saved. To our immense relief, the Russians replaced the Germans a few days later. But we couldn't relax for long, since we learned the Germans were returning. Our group of about ten vagabonds travelled to Lvov, which was still under Russian control, and I found a job as a stock-keeper at a factory.

The Russians were not bad fellows. They didn't want anything from us. They loved soccer and wanted to organize the factory workers into a soccer team. So as well as stock-keeping, I had the secondary role of organizing the team. I managed to get a message to my parents and fiancée, Genia, that I was okay, and they sent some parcels and money.

During 1939 and 1940, the Russians and Germans worked closely together. In Lvov, the Germans offered to repatriate anybody who had escaped from the Polish territories. Our Russian supervisor hid about twenty-five workers in an apartment, warning us not to go outdoors. Perplexed and afraid, we stayed put. That night, all those who had registered for repatriation were put on special transports to Siberia.

Living under false documents, I stayed in Lvov about eighteen months. Then, in 1941, the Russian-German war broke out, and the prophetic words of the Dresden professor rang again in my ears. A few brave souls had gone from Lvov to Vilnius or Kaunas, and thence to China. They had used their initiative and found a way out! Why hadn't I done the same?

Then chaos descended upon Lvov as the Germans embarked on a week-long spree of killing, terrorizing, raping, and robbing. My parents, who had moved to Bochnia, a town near Kraków, rescued me by sending a driver for me. Reunited with my parents and two sisters and brother in Bochnia, I started working in a Jewish factory, making brushes for the Germans. Mentally, I prepared for the day when I knew dramatic action would be necessary.

In August 1941, my parents were shipped to Belzec, a concentration camp, and I feared the worst. Now more than ever, I was determined to run away. Advised that the German employment office in Vienna would give me work, I

My brother Chaim

went there, gambling that the Nazis were satisfied that Austria was *Judenrein*. I sent for my fiancée, Genia, who, with her blue eyes and blonde hair, looked remarkably like a gentile. Equipped with false papers, money, and new clothes, I also attempted to pass myself off as a non-Jew. With my Jewish face, I knew I was taking a big chance not wearing the Star of David, but I didn't care. I found a job making fittings so railway cars could transport loose wheat, and Genia found work as a translator at an electronics factory. Although I was given a bed in the factory barracks, I secretly maintained my own apartment. For about a year, we had a perfect life in hiding.

One day, I was astonished to see a Jewish-looking girl walking openly in the street. "Are you Jewish?" I asked her. "Please don't be afraid, because I'm Jewish, too." She admitted that she was Jewish — and from Kraków! The story of how she had reached Vienna amazed me. In Kraków, the Germans had deported her parents in an *aktion*, she said. Gnawed by hunger, she snuck from the ghetto to the railroad station, where some drunken German soldiers approached her. "Good day. You're so beautiful, would you like to go with us to Vienna?" they asked. She replied, "Yes, I'll go, provided you give me something to eat." So they gave her bread and cheese, and together they boarded the train.

At each of the three border crossings between Kraków and Vienna, they hid her underneath the seat. When the border police asked if they had anything to declare, the soldiers replied, "Yes, but it's under the seat." The girl was frightened to death, but the inspectors, seeing that the soldiers were drunk, didn't bother to look. Upon reaching Vienna, the girl had gone to the police, of all places, and by some miracle, not suspecting she was Jewish, they helped her find work as a chambermaid. Eventually, she survived Auschwitz and other camps, married an ex-British soldier, an old

Genia and Alex Grossman in their mid-twenties

school friend of mine, and emigrated to Canada. I knew nothing of all this until I met the lady again at a dinner party in my own house in Toronto twenty years later. What an incredible coincidence.

After a year, my situation in Vienna suddenly became dangerous. The Germans had nabbed a fellow Jew to whom I had given some false papers and had traced the papers back to me. As I was returning to the barracks, some Polish women warned me that the Gestapo were waiting. That was the second time in my life that I ran away with no more than the shirt on my back. At Genia's apartment, I arranged my getaway. Being a wheeler-dealer, I had some business to conclude. For instance, one German officer, head of the employment office, had given me some money for a kilo of *speck*, a type of pork. Before I left, I instructed Genia to deliver the package of meat, which she faithfully did.

Assisted by my connections, I reached Budapest and then sent for my future wife. We were married there in a synagogue in 1944, with only my brother Chaim in attendance. By then, my parents, Henoch and Leah, were gone. I did not know for sure, but Belzec had a reputation as a death camp as bad as Auschwitz. As well, my sisters, Shanka and Gutka, were in the Kraków ghetto; both died later at Auschwitz. The only good news was that Chaim had joined us in Budapest. Being Polish nationals, we were well taken care of by the Polish government in exile, which had money for such a purpose. We were sent to work camps, but these hardly resembled the German concentration camps.

One day I met a high-placed Hungarian Jewish government official, Baron Denes Von Freudiger, whose brother had arranged our wedding. This baron led a privileged life, with a palatial apartment filled with treasures, even servants. When Genia and I were entertained there on the seventh day (*sheva boruchas*) after our wedding, we weren't sure which fork to use. The baron had even been to the United States and back, in 1942. Here was another guy with a false sense of security! Recalling the Dresden professor, I begged him to flee. Of course, he had all sorts of reasons why he couldn't leave, protesting just as my father had done. Later, fortunately for him, he was killed by a bomb. If he had ended up at Auschwitz, they would have given him the special treatment reserved for high-ranking officials.

If one dared to take a risk, it was possible to escape. I argued this point with nearly everybody. Since things seemed so hopeless, what was there to lose in at least trying to do something? But nobody wanted to hear it. They listened to the news every day, yet they didn't move! Paralyzed with fear, they preferred to deceive themselves into thinking the Germans were losing.

When the Germans penetrated Hungary, the Hungarian collaborators welcomed them as enthusiastically as we had welcomed the arrival of D-Day. The Jews were in danger. Genia was hired by the Jewish organization JIAS to smuggle people out of Budapest. Who would suspect that the beautiful blonde woman who escorted groups to the Romanian border was a Jew? She continued her work until 1944, when we ourselves tried to escape. Unfortunately, we aroused the suspicion of a streetcar conductor in a town on the Transylvanian border, who delivered us to the Gestapo. Thank God they took her for a Catholic, otherwise we would have been shot.

Placed in a Hungarian jail, I met Freddy Klein, a Jew from Temesvar, Romania, who was being daily questioned and tortured by an SS henchman wanting money. I counselled Freddy to tell the Gestapo goon that he could put a fair sum of money at his disposal if he could be taken to Temesvar.

"You're crazy!" the man protested. "If I say that, he will kill me!"

"So what have you got to lose!" I answered. "You're three-quarters dead already!"

He took my advice, and about ten days later they indeed took him to Temesvar, and he found an opportunity to save himself. As for me and my wife, we were shipped back to Budapest. For seven or eight months, well into 1945, we were prisoners of the Gestapo, permitted to live only because they did not know we were Jews. When Russian bombs started falling on Budapest, we were shipped back to Vienna and thrown first into a barracks-type jail, then a transport camp.

Soon the Germans released us, ordering us to work. Amazingly, we were brought to the very man to whom I had made good on my promise to deliver the kilo of *speck*! He was dumbfounded to see me — thank God, because he knew that I had once run from the Gestapo. Instead of exposing us, however, he helped us by sending us to work on a farm in a nearby town, Wiener Neustadt.

The Russians liberated the region in March 1945. Travelling by any conveyance available, we reached Budapest in April. The war ended in May, but on New Year's Eve, 1946, tragedy again struck my family. My brother Chaim, who had survived the war, had told us in December that he was going to be married. Returning to Poland, he and his two friends were killed in a car accident.

Our daughter Lilly was born in June 1946. We tried living in Prague, Kraków, and Paris. Finally settling in Belgium, I made some money in the coffee trade. After several years we arranged to come to Canada, once the Canadian consul accepted my assurances that we were not communists and that I would deposit a substantial sum of money in an account with the Royal Bank of Canada.

When we arrived here in January 1950, my wife was pregnant with our second child, George. It took some time for me to appreciate Toronto, which seemed like a backwater. Meanwhile, I went into the real-estate business with two partners, and our company became a big success.

When I think back about the game of Russian roulette we played to slip out of the clutches of the Nazis with just minutes to spare, I can scarcely believe it. But thankfully, I've always had good luck. Luck was vital in order to survive — and a willingness to take risks, to dare to act in the face of danger.

Standing in front of my childhood home in Kraków in 1987. I had left in 1939 intending to come home for lunch. Returning after all these years, I did not even bother to enter.

*Me at a Chanukah ball
dressed as a gypsy girl*

HELEN RODAK-IZSO

—⋊⋉—

The Last Chance to Remember

*"If the heavens were parchment, and the sea were ink,
there would not be enough of either to describe the atrocities of the Holocaust."*

I am a survivor of the Holocaust. That I have survived at all is simply a matter of chance.

The horrors began on March 19, 1944, when the German army marched into our country and into our home town, Košice, which was then known by its Hungarian name, Kassa. This was the Beginning of the End. No words can describe the dead silence, the numb fear.

The tragic day arrived when our street had to be emptied. How can anybody understand what it is to leave a home? A home where we were together, where we enjoyed meals, conversations, books — where once it mattered that the windows should be clean, that all manner of small and large problems be discussed and solved — where we were surrounded by affection and felt that nothing bad could happen?

I looked around to say goodbye to the familiar furniture, pictures, my old friend the grand piano, and took a last glance down at the garden, where the tulips and daffodils were nodding under the blue sky. The Hungarian policeman startled us, shouting, "Move already, go ahead. Your feet will never cross this threshold again." Even today I can still hear the ring of his south-Hungarian dialect.

Me at 17, 1932

Me and my family in 1943 (Back row, left to right: my sister, Olly; my brother, Leslie; me. Front row, left to right: my mother; my father)

We were homeless. They herded us to a brick factory with no walls. It was already dark and raining when we arrived and the place was crowded. "Make room for a new family," I heard someone say. Last night we were in our comfortable house, tonight we slept in the rain, crowded in with strange families. The next day was not any easier, with smoke and brick dust in our food and clothes. Among the most bitter and trying memories is the latrine, which was designed especially to humiliate us. It was in the open, the guards standing there all the while with rifles pointed. To see my parents endure these privations was unbearable, and they in turn were heroic in their attempts to protect us. I must confess that for me this part of our struggle is, and was, the darkest time, to see my parents subjected to such indignities. And there was no one to turn to for help.

On Thursday, June 2, 1944, we were ordered to leave the brick factory. First we had to undress in front of the police while the women searchers humiliated us looking for jewels. Then we were quick-marched away, hundreds of us, with no idea where we were going. I remember seeing the sparkle of diamonds in the mud. My dear father remarked quite quietly, "This is clearly the end." Since he had always been an optimist, these words were terrifying.

In the distance we spotted the cattle-cars waiting for us with open doors, and, to make matters worse, a heavy rain began to pour down on us. More than seventy-five people were ordered into each wagon. We took turns sitting on the floor in our wet clothes; we had no room to stretch out. There was a toilet pail around which we wrapped a sheet to allow a little privacy. We spent two days like this, without food, water, or rest. I remember my father saying, "There is no doubt where we are going."

At 2 P.M. on Sunday we arrived at Auschwitz, at the gate to hell marked "*Arbeit Macht Frei*." Prisoners in their striped clothes were waiting there to guide this mass of people into rows, five abreast. The men were separated from us before we knew it. My dear father was already some distance away, and the last I ever saw of him he was holding out a jar of jam, as if offering a sign of himself. With loud orders in German, we were shoved forward until we came to a halt in front of the god of these parts, the Angel of Death, Dr. Mengele. When he asked my dear mother her age and she answered truthfully, she was told to go to the left, my sister and I to the right. My mother looked back once more — I can see her face even now, in her navy silk kerchief, with a look of numb terror. I never saw her again. My sister and I found her kerchief the next

Left: My mother, Terez Friedman, 1935
Right: My father, Mark Friedman, 1935

day and cut it in two. We managed to save it for a year. An SS woman, whip in hand, gun in belt, and a stick in her boot, shouted, "*Sie verfluchte Juden! Loos! Loos!*" ("You damned cursed Jews! Go on, move, move!").

We were marched past barracks stretching as far as the eye could see, high watchtowers, and electrified barbed-wire fences. We passed a pile of logs where corpses were burned, because the gas chambers were working at full capacity. How could all this be happening in the open, under the blue sky, for all the world to see? Why didn't someone put a stop to this? Was it so morbid, so upsetting, that people preferred to look aside and go on with their lives?

Our march led us next to the "de-lousing" building. Here we found fifty to sixty girls, the last survivors of many thousands deported from Slovakia two years earlier. They were in terrible shape. Of course they no longer had any human feelings; they were simply zombies. One of these sad girls had the job of cutting my hair. How many heads had she done? She worked with no feeling, pulling my hair so hard it was very painful. "Just what did you think?" she said. "That you would escape the whole thing? While we were suffering for years already, you were still leading a normal life?"

Later, I was able to understand how she felt, how desperate, when we, the new victims, had arrived, because this meant the hoped for end was still not in sight.

After we were ordered to strip, we were a horrible sight — naked, with no hair. We could hardly recognize each other. German soldiers were walking in and out as if we didn't count as human any more. We stood there for hours — hungry, thirsty, and mentally exhausted. I saw shaved men marching by the window, and I searched in vain for my father, but it was impossible to distinguish one from another. Somehow all the figures and shapes blended together into one huge, grey body.

Late in the afternoon, we found ourselves in the shower. No soap. The water was handled by men, but they, too, didn't count us as women. Then our backs were marked in red with a big brush, and we were lined up to have numbers tattooed on our arms — but luckily they ran out of ink. Late at night, we finally found our barrack. I was desperate to lie down, anywhere, but it was too crowded. Hundreds of us were looking for a spot on the concrete floor of what was once a washroom. We leaned against one another until our minds went numb with exhaustion. After three days we were given some soup for the first time, one bowl for fifty people, just like animals.

It was mind-boggling how the Germans had the physical strength to inflict such barbarism on us, day after day, and all this in a country that once was a centre for culture and knowledge.

Next morning, thank goodness, we again left for the railway station, where a long row of cattle-cars was once more waiting with open doors. Since there was no food, we tried some grass. Hunger is a stern master and doesn't allow for pride, no matter how disciplined or educated you are. We dreamed about food. I remember arguing with my sister about whether a certain torte required thirteen or fourteen eggs, when we had no hope of seeing even one.

We arrived at Kaiserwold, which was a bit better. Here, we were given striped jackets and rags for our heads and could stretch out on wooden cots.

A lady from Vienna gave me a sewing needle. No thread yet, but it was a good feeling to have a friend, and a possession.

Then a bizarre incident occurred while I was working in a vegetable garden. An SS man bent down and plucked a piece of mint-like vegetable, which he handed me to taste. Then he ordered me into his office, guns hanging on the wall, and I sat on a chest that was probably full of ammunition. He brought me a bowl of soup made from the delicate vegetable, and insisted I finish it right then in front of him. If only I could have shared it with my sister. Was he intending to shoot me after this, and didn't he know what a torture

Top left: My maternal grandparents Rosa and Herman playing chess, with my uncle looking on. I remember the two of them often sitting at this table, he reading the newspaper, she doing her knitting.

Bottom left: Back row (left to right): Clara, Mother, Aunt Ella. Front row (left to right): Uncle Marci, my grandparents, Imi

Top right: Aunt Ella, Uncle Marci, and Mother

Bottom right: I took this shot of my nephews Ervinke and Imi. Sadly, Imi was to have his Bar Mitzvah in the ghetto.

Young Jewish men of Košice and neighbouring towns depart to forced-labour camps, c. 1942

it is for a starved body to eat more than a few spoonfuls? Afterwards he dismissed me, into the sunlight, dazed and sweating.

From Kaiserwold we were transported again, in roofless box cars, where for four days we were helplessly exposed to rain and blazing sun. I never knew if there would be a tomorrow. Kurbe, in Latvia, is where we spent the following weeks. Here, we worked in the forest, cutting down trees. We had no idea even how to begin to do this, but we learned quickly, always to the orders *"Loos! Loos!"* ("Go! Move on!"). One day in the forest I forgot myself and began to hum and whistle a Schubert song that I had often sung while playing the piano, although I never had a good voice. Suddenly the *Aufseherin* (female SS guard) was there demanding to know the meaning of this. I was prepared for the worst; I had seen people shot for less. But surprisingly she asked me to sing louder, and all of us had a moment's break to lean on our shovels and reminisce about our loved ones.

We were moved again – another cattle-car. Four days of torture like being in an oven – no room to stretch out even a little bit, kicking and pushing, nerves frayed beyond imagination. The new camp was Stutthof, which was like Auschwitz or worse. Here, we were not put to work, which made our lives even more unbearable. There was nothing to do but wait in fear for them to torture us or select new victims for extermination. When we left this cursed place after a few weeks, even the cattle train was better, almost welcome. Under the beautiful sky, birds flew in freedom over our heads.

In Glöwen, we worked again in the forest. I remember, after a rain, the wet grass, mushrooms, and wild flowers combined their scents to create a unique wild forest aroma. Every fall, when I smell that smell, I am reminded of those days in Glöwen.

On one occasion we decided to check our minds to see if they were still working. The assigned work that day was relaying fifty-kilogram bombs from one person to the next. As we passed each bomb along the line, we asked the person next to us a question, such as the name of an actor, play, or book. If the question was too difficult, the answer would be given on the next relay. Back at the barracks on a Sunday afternoon, we recited poems, and I remember telling stories of books I had read, because I have always had a love affair with books.

Me in 1945

Meanwhile, my life was nothing but hunger, thirst, and filth. Minute by minute I lived in abject terror. Almost every week they made those dreaded selections, and I never would know which side led to life or death.

One Saturday evening we left Glöwen for yet another journey into fear. We marched for three weeks, day and night. I heard bombs and air raids in the distance, and trees were on fire. I hid in ditches when the air raids came closer, and again the best food I could find was grass. The road was full of civilians: old people carrying bundles, families with their farm animals. It seemed as if the whole world was on the road, escorted by sirens and bombing.

All kinds of goods had been cast off along the way. I regretted I was too weak to carry a typewriter I found. I was frail and sick with dysentery. I did take the strings from a violin to serve as shoelaces. I remember feeling so light-headed that I had to force myself to step down harder to remind myself which way was up.

In Ravensbruck we were inexplicably given Red Cross parcels. They were like gifts from heaven. I couldn't believe my luck. I opened this treasure and turned over each neatly wrapped package in wonderment. Real, edible, untouched food — cocoa, instant coffee, crackers, biscuits. What a blessing.

But here at Ravensbruck it was clear the end was in sight. People had drifted here from many camps. I hoped in vain to find relatives. I saw stiff naked bodies thrown on a big pile and was afraid to look at them closely for fear I might recognize my mother's appendectomy scar.

Now we had to hit the road again, to join the parade of refugees looking for the end. It lasted about three weeks. I felt so light-headed that again I had to force myself to make firm contact with the ground with each step, otherwise a breeze might have lifted me up and I would be flying. We came to a hill overlooking a picturesque scene of a tranquil meadow and farmhouse – as though I had turned the page of a storybook to see a painting of an enchanted land. Like so many Goldilockses, we climbed down the hill and entered the house.

Nobody was home. The table was set for breakfast, the oven was warm, and there was a sitting room with soft chairs and bedrooms upstairs. The place spoke of a family life that we had lost, and we were completely mesmerized; it did not strike us that the occupants had departed only to take cover temporarily during an air raid. I washed with warm water, dressed myself in someone's clean farm clothes, and, I must confess, left my lice-infested striped uniform on the floor. My sister scrambled five eggs, but it was too much food too suddenly, and we couldn't eat it.

One by one we began to leave the farmhouse as it dawned on us that the family was likely to return. But we were not quick enough, and found ourselves face to face with the owners, who, in their anger, were terrifying. It was too much. We just walked away, incapable of caring any more. That night we lay down in wet grass as usual.

I was awakened by the sound of horses. Could it be possible? Yes, there stood a grey horse, and mounted on it was a Russian soldier. We hugged each other, we hugged the soldier, and even hugged the horse. We were liberated! This was May 2, 1945, in Muritz, just outside Hamburg. I had won the freedom for which I had hoped for so long, but it was difficult to handle. I was still insulated by that numbness so vital for survival.

Slowly my hair began to grow, and one of my comrades fashioned me a skirt from a pair of trousers. Now we were ready for the long trek back home. We walked to the railway station and sat on the concrete to wait. It didn't occur to us to use the benches. The train was a press of people all trying to get home, so rather than transfer, we had to stay on the train heading for Budapest. A few days later, we finally arrived at our home town. I had searched posters along the way listing the survivors, but nowhere could I find the names of my parents.

When the train pulled to a halt, the city seemed like a ghost town to my sister and me. A familiar figure approached in the gloom – our brother Leslie.

*The family fifty years later in Israel
(Left to right: me, my brother Alexander,
my sister Olly, my younger brother Leslie)*

With a heavy heart we climbed the steps to our dear parents' home. On the white door, unchanged, was the bronze nameplate *"Friedman Mark."* When the door opened, there was no one waiting for us. There was no need to hide our feelings any longer, and the three of us gave in to the anguish of our loss.

Only the heavy furniture remained. The Turkish rugs, we heard, had been taken away through the window. My grand piano was upside down and stuffed with straw.

My mother's favourite place in the house had been the balcony, a cosy spot with hanging flowerpots, and the day after our return a bird came to visit and began to build a nest among my mother's flowers. I watched while she made a home for her family. Flying in and out, she was such a cheerful sight.

I tell this story in memory of my father's family, the Friedmans, and my mother's family, the Moskovics.

Boarding the train in Germany on the start of our journey to Canada

ROSIE SILBERMAN ABELLA

Holocaust Imprint

M y parents spent four years in concentration camps. Their two-and-a-half-year-old son was killed, as were my father's parents and three brothers. My mother's family's factories were nationalized by the Polish government, and my father never got a chance to use the law degree he got before the war from the University of Kraków. When my mother was liberated from her concentration camp with my grandmother, she went back to the city she and my father had lived in before they were rounded up. She learned that my father, whom she had married two days after the Germans invaded Poland in September, 1939, was still in Theresienstadt. She "rode the rails" to Czechoslovakia, found the camp quarantined because of a typhoid epidemic, snuck in with a garbage detail, and rescued my father.

Father and me in Germany

They went to Stuttgart, Germany, with my grandmother, where I was born in 1946 and my sister was born in 1948. My father was president of the Jewish Community Council in Stuttgart and taught himself English when the Americans asked him to set up a system of legal services in Southwest Germany for displaced persons.

He tried for years to get into Canada. We finally arrived in 1950. My father was forty, my mother was thirty-three, and my grandmother over sixty. When

*With my parents, Jacob and
Fanny Silberman, in Germany*

we arrived in Toronto, my father went to the Law Society almost immediately
to see how he could qualify to practise law here. He was told only citizens
could practise law. It was a five-year delay he could not afford, so be became an
insurance agent.

My sister and I learned English from the other children in our neighbourhood, my mother learned it in night school, and my grandmother, who lived
with us, never spoke any language other than Yiddish. My sister and I went
to the public school around the corner, where there were only a few Jewish
students left after the massive migration in the fifties of Jewish families north
of Eglinton. In school we took piano lessons, and every Friday were given religious instruction in the New Testament by the minister of the local church.
Every Saturday we went for ballet and tap-dancing lessons, and, after we'd out-
grown the school piano teacher, for piano lessons. I sang Christmas carols in
the public-school choir every December and performed in Christmas plays.
On Sunday morning we went to the Shaarei Shomayim Synagogue, on St.
Clair Avenue, to learn Jewish history and traditions. On Friday afternoon after
school, we walked to the public library on Dufferin Street to get our three
books for the coming week. Every February we played piano in the Kiwanis
Music Festival.

Our best friend was often the only other Jewish girl in the class, but we
learned to make friends with everyone, even kids who called us "dirty Jews."

The neighbourhood and public-school culture felt seamless, and we were an integrated part of it.

Our parents expected us to do well in school and at piano. It was an expectation they didn't have to articulate — we simply understood that doing our best was part of the culture of the house. It never would have occurred to me not to try to measure up to my parents' unspoken standards. For their part, they always made me feel I *was* measuring up, and constantly encouraged and boosted me. It all felt so easy and wonderful and normal.

Then, slowly, in my mid-thirties, when my own children were in public school, I became conscious of the magic of my childhood and of my parents' strength. I realized that what seemed so normal to me was in fact extraordinary, and that the real miracle was how people who had lived through what my parents had lived through could provide so normal a home. The reality of all the stories they told me suddenly seemed to work its way down from my brain into my emotions. And once the stories about Europe I'd heard since childhood were transformed from calm narrative into soul-searing understanding, I was never the same again.

With my sister, Toni, in Germany

The home my parents created with my grandmother in Canada was joyful, optimistic, and fearless. They told me everything was possible and acted as if they meant it. They transformed their pain into hope, and handed it unconditionally to my sister and me. They never told me what the Holocaust meant, but they never had to. In their lives were all the lessons I needed to learn.

For me, as a woman deeply marked by her family's past, and as one who holds her parents in awe for their persistence in rebuilding healthy lives, I find I am shaped in two fundamental ways by the Holocaust. The first is that I feel an obligation to repay them for the efforts they made to reconstruct their lives, and to prove that it was worth their effort. Most survivors derived the energy and sustenance to carry on from their hope of guaranteeing for their children a life free from pain.

They succeeded, and we are a spoiled generation — our lives have not been horribly uprooted, nor did we have to bear witness to parents, children, and spouses dying cruelly and unnaturally. But as people free from this experience, we repay our parents' love by drawing from it the strength to contribute our energies and talents to society generally and to the Jewish community of which we are a part. With strength comes a capacity for generosity, and we must generously return in our various communities the investment our parents made, by

With Irving Abella on our wedding day, December 8, 1968

insisting on vigorous regard for the rights of others, by living our lives proud of our Jewishness, and by keeping alive the memories of those who themselves never had the chance to fulfil their potential. We have the gift of survivorship, and it both enables and obliges us to live our lives to the limit of our abilities. We have undoubtedly the right to live private lives, but we have a fundamental sense, too, that we must make a public contribution, in whatever way we can.

The second major influence I have felt is even more profoundly affecting. I take no one and nothing for granted. One comes away from the history of the Holocaust with a driving urgency for life. Having watched a whole generation intolerably interrupted in mid-life, one learns to appreciate intensely the fragility and temporal limitations of our own lives. The result is a compelling need to make the most of the opportunities one is given, and to value, cherish, and nurture the people one loves. It is not an unbridled drive — it is firmly circumscribed by the values one embraces.

If anything, the sense of fairness and decency rooted in Jewish tradition is heightened in those of us who feel the weight of history. We live not only for ourselves, but to honour our ancestors, by living with courage, integrity, and compassion. There is no competition with others; the competition is with time.

We – those who have survived – are an accident of history but can validate the accident on behalf of those millions who cannot. The memory must never die; we and our children and our children's children must do everything in our power to keep it alive, as a source of personal inspiration, of commitment, of justice, and of pride in who we are.

We must fear nothing but injustice; value little more than integrity; forgive everything but indifference.

These values the world forgot for one horrible moment, and we the survivors, in honour and memory of those who were its victims, must pledge to translate their and our loss into a fierce commitment never to let indifference overcome justice or integrity.

ABOUT THE CONTRIBUTORS

———— >‹‹ ————

IRVING ABELLA was born, raised, and educated within blocks of the geographic heart of Toronto's Jewish community at Spadina and College. He is a professor of Canadian and Jewish history at York University and is the author or co-author of over seventy-five articles and eight books, including *None Is Too Many: Canada and the Jews of Europe, 1933-1948*, and *A Coat of Many Colours: Two Centuries of Jewish Life in Canada*. A past president of the Canadian Jewish Congress and of Canadian Professors for Peace in the Middle East, he is presently chair of the Commission of Jewish Continuity and Identity, of the Council of Jewish Federations of Canada, and of the War Crimes Committee of the Canadian Jewish Congress.

ROSIE SILBERMAN ABELLA graduated from the University of Toronto Law School in 1970 and practised civil and criminal litigation until her appointment to the Family Court Bench in 1976, when she became the first Jewish woman to be made a judge in Canada. She was a member of the Ontario Human Rights Commission, chaired the Ontario Labour Relations Board and the Ontario Law Reform Commission, and was sole commissioner of the Royal Commission on Equality in Employment. She was a Visiting Professor at the McGill Law School for several years and has written four books and over sixty articles on a variety of legal subjects. She has her ARCT in piano and sixteen honorary doctorates. In 1992 she was appointed to the Ontario Court of Appeal.

She and her husband, Irving Abella, have two sons – Jacob, born in 1973, and Zachary, born in 1976.

MARY MANOVILLE BECK was born on February 28, 1936, in Budapest, Hungary. She survived the Second World War in Hungary and emigrated to Vienna in 1948, where she attended school. She also spent one year at a boarding school in England. Mary Beck arrived in Canada in 1952 with her parents and lives in Toronto.

JOE BERMAN was born in Elmira, Ontario, in 1922 to Morris and Mary. After studying engineering at the University of Toronto, he served as a lieutenant in the Royal Navy.

Joe Berman was a founding partner in the Cadillac Fairview Corporation. He has served on many government advisory boards and presented briefs including revisions to housing and building acts and the Bryce Commission on Corporation Concentration. He has served on the boards of the Reena Foundation, the Technion of Haifa, Aish Hatorah, UJA, Temple Sinai, and the United Jewish Welfare.

Joe and Helen Berman say they are proudest of their six children, twenty-one grandchildren, and five great-grandchildren, with three more on the way, G-d willing.

LOU BREGMAN, Toronto-born restaurant entrepreneur and business man extraordinaire, revolutionized the bagel industry in Toronto by opening the city's first bagel bakery restaurant, The Bagel King. His other successful ventures have included The Pie Tree, Bregman's Bakery Restaurant, Mmmuffins, Michel's Baguette, and Second Cup.

Lou has been married for forty-three years to Yetta Bregman. Together they have raised four wonderful children and are the proud grandparents of six lovely grandchildren. When he's not at the office, Lou's favourite pastime is having a cup of coffee and a bagel that someone else has made, for a change.

CHARLES R. BRONFMAN, a native Montrealer, is a graduate of McGill University. He is Co-Chairman and Chairman of the Executive Committee of the Seagram Company Ltd.

He also serves as Chairman of Claridge Israel Inc., and is Chairman of the Board of the Trustees of McGill Institute for the Study of Canada and of the *Jerusalem Report*. He is a member of many boards, including that of the Power Corporation of Canada, the *Canadian Jewish News*, and the Washington Institute for Near East Policy.

Mr. Bronfman's many community involvements include being Chairman and Founder of the CRB Foundation. The foundation works to enhance Jewish and Canadian heritage and has been a driving force behind "The Israel Experience," a program encouraging youth and young adults to connect to Israel through personal visits as a part of community programs. Mr. Bronfman also served as Chairman of the Montreal Expos from 1968 to 1990.

In 1992 Mr. Bronfman was made a Companion of the Order of Canada and a Member of the Queen's Privy Council for Canada.

BEN DUNKELMAN was born on June 26, 1913, into the prominent Toronto family of Rose and David Dunkelman. On his seventeenth birthday, Ben travelled to Israel and has been an active Zionist ever since.

As a major in the Queens Own Rifles, Ben received the DSO for his role in clearing the Hochwald in World War II. In 1948 he returned to Israel to command the 7th Brigade and played a critical role in the liberation of Israel. These events are chronicled in his autobiography *Dual Allegiance*, first published in 1976.

He has distinguished himself in Canada as an entrepreneur in many fields, from President of Tip Top Tailors to progenitor of the Constellation Hotel, the Cloverdale Shopping Centre, the Dunkelman Gallery, Dunkelman's Fine Dining, and the Daily Planet.

Avid outdoorsman and artist, Ben also enjoys spending his leisure time with his six children, his grandchildren, and with Yael, his wife of nearly fifty years.

BEATRICE FISCHER. Born: Woodstock, Ontario. Educated: Princess School; Central Public School; Woodstock Collegiate Inst.; Sir George Williams, Montreal; Cornell University. Best working experiences: Magazine Digest; Editorial Associates and International Labour Office magazine, Montreal; Director Advertising and Publicity, 20th Century Theatre Corp; Special Projects Officer, Royal Ontario Museum, Toronto. Best community projects: Amadeus String Ensemble; Opera Atelier Board; Habima Theatre, Israel. Adornments to my life: five children, five partners, five grandchildren, four siblings. Memory of my splendid husband Dr. Martin Fischer: a superb collection of RCMP kitsch.

BILL GOLD arrived in Toronto from England at six months of age. As a child, he earned a host of medals for baseball, none for school.

In 1934 he married Lil Gallander, one of the lovely Gallander girls. They have two beautiful daughters, Janice and Marsha, and four grandchildren. After a successful career at second base, he took to selling beer, first for the now extinct Dominion Breweries and then from his own hotels.

Bill Gold is currently enjoying his old age with Lil and their family.

MARTIN GOLDFARB was born in Toronto and has always lived there. He graduated from the University of Toronto with a master's in sociology in 1966. He shares authorship of *Marching to a Different Drummer: An Essay on the Liberals and Conservatives in Convention*, published in 1988. He is a student of behaviour and a business executive. He sits on several corporate boards, including that of the Goldfarb Corporation.

He currently serves on the Board of Governors of York University and is a past director of the Toronto Symphony, the Canadian Opera Company, the Shaw Festival, and the Canadian Council of Christians and Jews.

He and his wife, Joan, have five children.

EDWIN A. GOODMAN was born in Toronto during the great flu epidemic of 1918 and was schooled at Clinton Public School, Harbord Collegiate, the University of Toronto, and Osgoode Hall.

In the Second World War, he fought with the Fort Garry Horse and was wounded twice. He then entered his father's law practice, and today the firm has 220 lawyers.

Edwin Goodman married the lovely Suzie Gross (now deceased) and became the father of two beautiful daughters, Joanne (now deceased) and Diane, who gave the world Myles Samuel in September, 1996. He is now married to Joan Thompson, a fine lady with a Jewish heart.

After law, his chief interest is politics, and he is a former National Chairman of the Progressive Conservative Party. He is also a former president of the National Ballet and is Chairman of the Royal Ontario Museum. His spare time is devoted to Zionist endeavours.

SHIRLEY GRANOVSKY (née Rockfeld) was born in Toronto on January 12, 1924. She was raised on Huron Street along with two younger sisters. She attended Orde St. School and Central Commerce. Upon graduation she worked for Albert White as a bookkeeper. During the war years, she worked as a secretary at the Draft Board.

She married Philip Granovsky in 1946 and shortly afterward moved to Los Angeles, where a daughter and son were born. The family remained in Los Angeles for three and a half years. After returning to Toronto, she gave birth to another son and daughter. She worked along with her husband in communal endeavours, acting as hostess to the many meetings that were held in their home. She counts as her greatest accomplishments a very successful marriage and the raising of four decent, caring children.

ALEX GROSSMAN was born in 1919 in Kraków, Poland. He and his wife, Genia, survived the Holocaust and came to Toronto in 1950. He is President of the successful real estate company Belmont Properties. He served for many years as National Chairman of the Board of Israel Bonds in Canada and is now Honorary Chairman. Alex was a co-founder of Massuah, a Holocaust education centre in Israel, which he calls his "biggest accomplishment" and where he remains Chairman. He is also active with UJA, The Sshaare Tzedec Hospital Foundation, where he is Chairman, the Jewish Community Centre, the Baycrest Centre, and the Mount Sinai Hospital.

He and Genia have two children and four grandchildren.

ETHEL HARRIS was born and grew up in Toronto. She holds a master's degree in political science and economics and another in English language and literature.

After raising her family of three children, she became a writer, and in 1990 published *The King and The Flea*, a collection of Jewish folk tales, and in 1994 *A Rage of Poppies*, a book of poems. Her work has appeared in various Canadian literary magazines, including *Matrix*, *Canadian Author and Bookman*, *Quarry*, and *Fireweed*.

Ethel Harris is now a full-time painter. Her premier exhibition took place in the spring of 1997 at the Rebecca Gallery in Toronto.

MILTON HARRIS grew up in London, Ontario, and in 1969 moved to Toronto, where he now lives.

He is the founder and chief executive officer of the Harris Steel Group. He has served as president of the Toronto Jewish Congress, the Canadian Jewish Congress, and as chairman of the finance committee of the federal Liberal Party of Canada. In adittion, he has been a member of the Senate of the University of Western Ontario and of the boards of Air Canada and Canadair.

Milton Harris is an Officer of the Order of Canada.

BEN KAYFETZ, born in Toronto, taught high school after graduating from the University of Toronto. From 1945 to 1947 he was with the control commission of Germany, then was on staff of the Canadian Jewish Congress as director of its community relations program until 1985. Ben is a former Canadian correspondent for the Jewish Telegraphic Agency and the *Jewish Chronicle* of London, England. He has written many articles on Jewish history. His awards include the Samuel Bronfman Medal and the Order of Canada.

Ben is married to Eva (Silver), and they have three daughters and five grandchildren.

JULIA KOSCHITZKY's whole life has been steeped in yiddishkeit, in taking an active part in Jewish communal life. She is chairman of the board of the United Israel Appeal of Canada, and she serves on the boards of the Jewish Agency for Israel and the *Canadian Jewish News*. In the past she has chaired UJA campaigns and the Keren Hayesod World Board of Trustees.

In 1990 she received the Woman of Valour Award, in 1993 the Commonwealth Confederation Medal, and in 1994 the Jerusalem Award.

Julia and Henry Koschitzky have eight grandchildren.

ARLENE PERLY RAE has been very active in public life. She reviewed children's books in the *Toronto Star* for seven years and has now written *Everybody's Favourites*, an intimate survey of the wide variety of literature that influenced Canadians as young readers. She is chief judge of the Mr. Christie Book Awards, and is active with several organizations that promote literacy, including World Literacy of Canada. She is co-owner of Crescent Communications. Her volunteer activities are diverse, ranging from anti-racism initiatives at two universities, to fundraising for various causes, to promoting a healthy progressive community through her speeches and writing assignments.

HELEN RODAK-IZSO (née Friedman) was born in 1915 in Košice, Slovakia (then Hungary), and married her childhood sweetheart in 1942. He was sent to a Russian labour camp with the army and perished there. From April 1944 to the end of the war, Helen was transported to twelve concentration camps.

In 1948, she married Joseph Rodak and they emigrated to Canada. She has two sons, George Avie and Paul, two daughters-in-law, Jean and Bonnie, and five grandchildren, Rina, Terri, Michelle, Jillian, and Shane, who are the light of her life.

For twenty-five years, Helen has worked in the University of Toronto Robarts Library among her treasured books, and her story here is excerpted from her writings on her Holocaust experiences.

FRED SHARF entered his father's wholesale fruit and vegetable business in the Ontario Food Terminal after returning from serving overseas with the Canadian Army.

After six years of getting up at 3:30 A.M., six days a week, he decided that he did not want to do this for the rest of his life, and convinced his father to sell the business.

With his brother and brother-in-law, Fred went into the building business and after two years teamed up with three others to start Wycliffe Homes Ltd., which was very successful from its inception.

The partnership spawned many other businesses, including the Pickle Barrel and Bloomsbury restaurant chain, the Mayfair Tennis Club, etc., etc.

Fred and his wife, Rosslyn, have two children and five grandchildren.

ROSALIE WISE SHARP grew up in Toronto, the only Jew in the neighbourhood. Married to Isadore Sharp for forty-two years, she has four sons, Jordan, Gregory, Christopher, and Anthony; two daughters-in-law, Ann and Mary; three grandchildren, Emily, Julia, and Aaron; and two granddogs.

Rosalie won the Lieutenant Governor's Medal at the Ontario College of Art and Design, where she now chairs the board of trustees. An interior designer, she best enjoys drawing up restaurants. In her spare time she collects antique British pottery and porcelain (this has gotten out of hand), sings (poorly), dances (fair), and plays bridge (middling).

JOSEPH M. TANENBAUM, entrepreneur and philanthropist, was born in Toronto and studied engineering at the University of Toronto.

He is Chairman of the Art Gallery of Ontario, and a director of the Sunnybrook Medical Centre, the Sunnybrook Cancer Centre, the University of Toronto, the Canadian Opera Company, and the Canadian Psychiatric Research Foundation.

He is a Member of the Order of Canada and is a recipient of the Commander's Cross of the Order of Merit of the Sovereign Order of Malta, the Lescarbot Award, the Ontario Association of Art Galleries Partner/Individual Award, and the University of Toronto Arbor Award.

He and his wife, Toby, have five children – Michael, Alan, Martin, Susan, and Robert. They presently reside in Toronto.

MORLEY TORGOV, born in 1927 in Sault Ste. Marie, is the author of four books, two of which, *A Good Place to Come From* and *The Outside Chance of Maximilian Glick*, were awarded the Leacock Medal for Humour. His fourth book, *St. Farb's Day*, received a City of Toronto Book Award and the Jewish Fiction Book Award.

Morley Torgov has practised law in Toronto since 1954 and holds an honorary doctorate in Literature from Laurentian University. He is married to Anna Pearl Cohen of St. Catharines and has two children and four grandchildren. He is currently writing a new novel and a thick volume of post-dated cheques.

IRVING UNGERMAN, upon his return in 1945 from serving overseas with the RCAF, kissed Canadian soil and at that moment realized land cannot be replaced! From then on he invested in real estate, beginning with the purchase of a tract of land for four dollars a running foot in the vicinity of Dufferin and Wilson avenues.

From there, he forged ahead in the poultry business, real estate, building, boxing, sport promotions (Chuvalo, Ali, Evel Knievel) and politics. He and his wife, Sylvia, have also always been avid collectors of Canadian Art.

Irving Ungerman has tremendous pride in being a Canadian citizen. He is confident that his being a "self-made man" is a result of the enterprising spirit of Canada and his dedication to excellence.

FRED WEINBERG, M.D., F.R.C.P.(C), F.A.A.P., is a senior physician at the Hospital for Sick Children in Toronto. His referral practice is confined to neurological problems such as attention deficit disorder. He has published over fifty articles on Judaica in English and Yiddish and wrote the catalogue text for the Royal Ontario Museum's "Precious Legacy" exhibition from Prague. He was a founder of the Cecil Roth Museum Collection at Toronto's Beth Tzedec Congregation, where he was president for three years. He has contributed to journals in his fields of neurology, museology, and history.

He and his wife, Joy Cherry, their four wonderful children, their children's spouses, and their four grandchildren, all live in Toronto. He is currently doing less collecting of objects and more collecting of friends.

MICHAEL WEX, the sole known descendant of Rebbes Wolf Strykover and Avremele Tshekhanover to have been born in Lethbridge, Alberta, is a bon vivant, raconteur, and occasional teacher of Yiddish. Educated first in yeshivas, later at the University of Toronto, this former specialist in Old and Middle English literature was a fellow of Massey College, where he can be loosely described as having been Robertson Davies' housemate. He is the author of the novel *Shlepping the Exile* and of three stage-shows – *God in Paris*, *Judenverwolkung*, and *Sex in Yiddish* - which have lately been playing in Germany.

LARRY ZOLF has been immersed in Canadian politics all his life. He was born and raised in North End Winnipeg, the hotbed of general strikes and Canadian socialism, and in graduate school did his thesis on the Liberal Party of Ontario and Canada. After university, he engaged in trade union politics for two years.

Since joining the CBC in 1962, Larry Zolf has covered literally dozens of conventions, nominations, elections, and other political events. In particular, Larry has been heavily involved in controversial programming for the CBC, and for his part in "This Hour Has Seven Days," Larry was fired by the president of the corporation. His political commentary is currently featured in "Inside Zolf" on CBC Newsworld's internet service.

With thanks to the team — Alex Schultz, Nomi Morris, Kong Njo,
Avie Bennett, Isadore Sharp — and to McClelland & Stewart for
publishing this book as a public service.
— Rosalie Wise Sharp

A Note on Transliteration

Some say Zeyda, and some say Zaida. On the other hand, we have *machen* (to make), or should
it be *makhen*? Since dictionaries vary, I consulted my authority, Ben Kayfetz, who has given his
hechsher (stamp of approval) to use my personal preference.   R. S.

Irving Abella   Shirley Granovsky   Martin Goldfarb   Joe Berman   B

Beatrice Fischer   Larry Zolf   Fred Sharf   Michael Wex   Mo

Charles Bronfman   Milt Harris   Ethel Harris   Rosalie Sharp   M